How to Really be a Brit

Emerging from the depths of Twitter on an auspicious April Fool's Day in 2021, No Context Brits swiftly garnered an ardent following of over 1.8 million devotees. This iconic account weaves an intricate tapestry of relatable British culture memes, often leaving viewers both baffled and amused by their lack of context.

How to Really be a Brit

The Unofficial Citizenship Test

No Context Brits

VIKING

an imprint of

PENGUIN BOOKS

VIKING

UK | USA | Canada | Ireland | Australia
India | New Zealand | South Africa

Viking is part of the Penguin Random House group of companies
whose addresses can be found at global.penguinrandomhouse.com.

First published 2023
001

Copyright © No Context Brits, 2023

The moral right of the author has been asserted

Set in 9.2/14.75pt Real Text Pro
Typeset by Jouve (UK), Milton Keynes
Printed and bound in Great Britain by Clays Ltd, Elcograf S.p.A.

The authorized representative in the EEA is Penguin Random House Ireland,
Morrison Chambers, 32 Nassau Street, Dublin D02 YH68

A CIP catalogue record for this book is available from the British Library

ISBN: 978-0-241-66712-5

www.greenpenguin.co.uk

MIX
Paper | Supporting
responsible forestry
FSC® C018179

Penguin Random House is committed to a
sustainable future for our business, our readers
and our planet. This book is made from Forest
Stewardship Council® certified paper.

For Rocco and Cali Rae

Contents

Contents

Introduction

Do you know what year the Harrier jump jet was developed?
What about the name of the first king of Scotland, or the director
   of Chariots of Fire?
Surely you must know the contents of the 1689 Bill of Rights?!

If you're a true-blue, tea-drinking, Union Jack-waving, Queen-curtseying, Tesco Club Card-carrying Brit, you do. At least, so says the Home Office. These questions and more like them are among those posed by the Life in the UK test, taken by those applying for settlement in Britain or for citizenship. Every year some 177,000 people sit the test, seeking to prove their grasp of British society, traditions and values just so that they can stay here for ever.

Most will have lived here for years already; they may well have never known any other home. But if they are to be free to remain indefinitely in the eyes of the Home Office, they must be able to tell their M6 from their M1, their ploughman's sandwich from their builder's tea, their Lancasters from their Yorks. (Those are red roses versus white. Just FYI.)

The test is the final hurdle in the costly and time-consuming process to becoming a Brit, after the lengthy application and even lengthier paperwork to prove your English language comprehension skills. (Though you can ask to sit the test in Welsh or Scottish Gaelic, if you would prefer.)

Alessandro Mascellino, a British-Italian journalist who wrote

3

the foreword to the 2022 edition of the *Life in the UK Test: Handbook*, said that he was 'initially shocked by the legal requirements and procedures'. The process of becoming an Italian citizen is more straightforward – and they have sunshine, fresh pasta and tomatoes that actually taste of tomatoes.

In a way, Mascellino valiantly suggested – with the determined optimism of a group of Brits planning a barbecue in May – reaching the milestone of the Life in the UK test is good news: it means that only twenty-four multiple-choice questions stand between you and the right to remain in the UK indefinitely.

On the other hand, it means you could fall short of the appropriate bar for Britishness for inadequate knowledge of the Picts – or, Heaven forbid, whether Hallowe'en lanterns are carved out of A) melons, B) pineapples, C) coconuts or D) pumpkins. (Look, all of us can get flustered under pressure.)

That's on top of the indignity of having to pay fifty quid to sit the test in the first place, not to mention the cost of having to take time off work or travel to your closest centre. You can't count on the Home Office to make it easy for you.

In fact, to prove yourself officially certified for life in the UK, you must answer eighteen of those twenty-four correctly. That's a pass rate of 75 per cent – what would be, for a university paper, an exceptional mark.

So it's perhaps no surprise that, of those 177,000 people who sit the test every year, two in ten fail – maybe because they don't know whether the Scottish New Year celebration is called Hogmanay or Hopmanay, or the origins of 'the first farmers'.

Many of the facts that the Home Office considers 'essential knowledge' for Life in the UK seem arbitrary and bizarre. For example, applicants 'are advised to know about Scottish courts even if you are taking the test in London' – it's hard to fathom why. You are also reassured that you won't be asked dates of birth or death – but you might be asked for the years in which particular bits of legislation were passed.

On the plus side, with all these fun facts at your disposal, you are bound to be a welcome addition to any pub quiz team in the future.

Between the odd scope of the test and the secrecy that surrounds it – the handbook relies on first-person accounts from people who've sat it, like crib sheets being left in the bathroom stalls – it is hard to escape the impression that the government doesn't want to make any more Brits. Or maybe it's that they want only a particular kind.

These questions, attempting to articulate what makes Britain and Brits so very British, without any context, often prompt questions of their own, like: Who says? Whose Britain? Who's British?

The popular image of Britain and Britishness that's often held up – of weather-chatting, cricket-playing, history-loving, mostly pasty-white Brits – isn't true for all of us. It's maybe not even true for most of us.

Often, when people talk about 'Britain' – whether they're misty-eyed, or seeing red – they're actually talking about England in particular, and maybe even just London.

The fact is, the UK reflected by the Life in the UK test is increasingly less relevant – if, indeed, it ever existed. Consider the change we've seen in the lifetime of just one person (albeit one with a God-given right to reign, and many lovely hats): the late Queen Elizabeth II.

When Her Majesty began her reign, in February 1952, Britain was a very different place. Clothes had just come off coupons, but food was still rationed. Phone calls were still made via an operator. There were only about 3.25 million television sets in the country, with just one channel – and they cost the equivalent of about two months' wages.

In recent years especially, change has seemed to be coming faster – and often more furiously.

In 2016, after a deeply divisive campaign, Britons voted to leave the European Union: a watershed moment that meant walking away from a political ally of nearly half a century's standing. After a challenging negotiation, to put it lightly, we finally got around to actually exiting four years (and three prime ministers) later, in January 2020.

By then, yet more ruptures had emerged in British society, challenging the two images of its society as equal and its history as glorious. The Windrush scandal in 2018 highlighted those British subjects who were disenfranchised, wrongly detained and even deported from the UK after having arrived from mostly Caribbean countries before 1973.

Likewise, more recently, awareness has been raised of those people who were bought and sold and brought to Britain against their will, or who otherwise had their autonomy overruled in the name of empire. After the global Black Lives Matter protests in 2020, a statue of slave trader Edward Colston in Bristol was toppled by activists.

A reckoning over Britain's past, and the costs of slavery, colonialism and empire – many of which continue to be deeply felt today – is ongoing.

The meaning of the monarchy itself – as straightforwardly a symbol of Great Britain as there is – has likewise been tested. On 8 September 2022, at the venerable age of ninety-six, Queen

Elizabeth II died – and a vision of Britain that many in this country have clung to for the best part of a century died with her.

Now, having once 'ruled the waves', we really may be finding ourselves in uncharted waters, ruled by a king known best to us as a big fan of homoeopathy and his triumphing side-chick as queen.

But even before the once-in-a-lifetime change in monarch, the royal family seemed increasingly in royal trouble. In 2020, Prince Harry and Meghan Markle made a break for it across the Atlantic, trading their God-given gilded cage for the relatively more permissive one of Hollywood.

Since then they have made up for their years of being silent – or silenced – by speaking out, in so many hours of footage, and tens of thousands of words, about alleged tensions and infighting within the Windsors. The popularity of the TV series *The Crown* has likewise made us feel like we've got front-row seats to the drama.

All of this has challenged and expanded our sense of British exceptionalism and our (always shonky) association of Britain with quaint images of tea and crumpets, corgis and cricket. Of course, it's never really stood up to scrutiny – but many people treasured it, all the same.

More and more, these days, these gaps and omissions are becoming harder to ignore, and what has long been taken for granted as common knowledge is being questioned. Achievements that might have been help up as proof that Britain is truly great are being looked at anew, like the fact that Britain abolished slavery – but only after many years of profiting and great pressure from enslaved people themselves.

Even the citizenship test has been forced, in some ways, to move with the times: the first virtual ceremony held in July 2020 as a result of the coronavirus pandemic. Pressure has also been mounting for it to be amended to reflect these unprecedented times – and revisit the ones that came before.

In the summer of 2020, nearly 200 historians called on the Home Office to remove the history element of the UK citizenship test. They said its representation of slavery and empire was 'misleading and false' – for example its inference that the transition from empire to Commonwealth was pretty orderly, actually, just a case of handing back independence to all those countries it was taken from by force . . .

So much has changed about Britain, as well as the way we think of it, that it's more or less transformed within the lifetime of just one individual.

Over the course of Queen Elizabeth's seventy-year reign, the number of people living in the UK grew by a whole 17 million – from just over 50 million in 1952 to just over 67 million in 2021. That increase has overwhelmingly been the result of immigration. (The birth rate has dropped to record-low levels. Does no one want to lie back and think of England any more?)

It goes to show the number of people wanting to live here, those who now consider Britain home and think of themselves as part of its life and culture – who might now be fighting for the right to remain, or seeking to make it official with citizenship.

Yet even as what we mean by Britain and Britishness is in flux – to the point that we're getting new coins with a bloke on them – aspiring Brits are still being asked about Handel's compositions for King George I and the number of Oscar wins for *Wallace and Gromit*.

The Home Office says that the Life in the UK test is 'designed to support cultural integration' and 'give greater prominence to British values and principles expected of those wishing to call the UK their permanent home'. It shows that the purpose is not just about reflecting Britain as it is: it's about upholding a particular vision of it too.

With the test, the government is effectively telling aspiring Britons that if you want to consider yourself 'one of us', you must not only know that Jane Austen was an eighteenth-century author but that her novels were concerned with 'marriage and family relationships' (to give the pretty reductive analysis in the *Life in the UK Test: Handbook*).

The kicker is that many born-and-bred Britons don't know the answers to these questions themselves – but, blessed with the indefinite right to remain by the circumstances of their birth, they don't have to.

It reveals the double standard embedded in the very premise of the test. 'Knowledge and understanding of British values is vital for those who wish to make the UK their home,' said then immigration minister Caroline Nokes in 2019. But knowing 'when was the hovercraft invented' has little to do with values, and even less to do with day-to-day life here – certainly much less than what happened on *Love Island* last night.

'I want everyone who comes here and makes their lives here to be, and to feel, British,' said Boris Johnson around the same time, during the Tory leadership race. Except the bar for being and feeling British is higher for people who weren't born here than it is for those who were.

Migrants need to have had unbroken leave to remain for a full decade before they can be officially recognized as permanently settled; many can't afford the costs of cementing their citizenship, putting them at risk of deportation. Meanwhile, those who set the rules don't feel obliged to follow them.

In 2012, then prime minister David Cameron was posed some

sample citizenship test questions on air by late-night TV host David Letterman. He got an embarrassing number wrong, actually proving stronger on American history. (Even more embarrassingly: Cameron had asked Letterman to have him on the show.)

But when the PM can't say who wrote the music for 'Rule Britannia', or the English translation of 'Magna Carta' when representing Britain on foreign soil and on live TV, he still gets to go home and run the country and force a vote on whether to leave or remain in the European Union.

Since Brexit, many self-identifying Britons have already been forced to leave, while those who might have dreamed of one day becoming Brits have abandoned hope. At time of writing, people across the countries are striking for a fairer, more functional Britain – the kind of place, in fact, that the Home Office's test claims to be welcoming you to.

It's undeniable that Britain and what it means to be a Brit is changing – but then, it always has been.

This alternative citizenship test aims to celebrate the many sides and aspects of Britishness: the ones we somehow all know, no matter where we might live on the planet; the ones that might come as a surprise to those who have spent all their lives here; and the ones that our government might not be so keen to lead with to new arrivals.

It's not a test that seeks to trip people up for not being British enough, or to make fun of them for being too British, or to rank one version over another. That is to say, it sets out to put Brits into context.

1. Weather

Ah, our national preoccupation. No matter how turbulent the times or divisive the headlines, you can always count on being able to connect with your fellow Brit on the subject of the atmosphere and weather conditions.

Bit chilly, isn't it? . . . It's blowing a gale out there! . . . Quite mild for this time of year . . . It's overcast . . . It's close . . . Nice day for it . . . And I didn't pack my umbrella . . . Bloody weather!

If that seems like an exaggeration, consider this: according to a national survey of England by the Social Issues Research Centre, 'at any given moment, at least a third of the population are probably talking about the weather'. (Unsurprisingly, the Scots, Welsh and Irish are made of sturdier stuff.)

We were doing it all the way back in the eighteenth century, too, with essayist Samuel Johnson observing that 'when two Englishmen meet, their first talk is of the weather'. At least it never gets boring, right?

If anything, it is becoming more fraught. The year 2022 was the hottest in the UK on record, with an average temperature of over 10 degrees Celsius recorded for the first time.

Heat that we've typically chased to the Continent is now coming to meet us at home – and it seems we've got mixed feelings about it. A YouGov survey of 4,700 Brits found that 58 per cent 'did not enjoy' the August 2022 heatwave.

Maybe 30-degree days are like squid in salads, topless

sunbathing and statement headwear: something we enjoy on holiday but might not bring home with us. As it is, the Met Office warns, we'd better get used to it.

At the least there'll be plenty for us to talk about.

A. 188

Questions

1. By what name is Anticyclone Hartmut better known?

□ **A)** The Beast from the East

□ **B)** The Test from the West

□ **C)** The Mouth of the South

□ **D)** The Hoolie from the Hebrides

2. If it's true that the Inuits have at least fifty words for snow, we Brits have at least as many for rain. What is the appropriate term for a prolonged period of really heavy rain?

□ **A)** Downpour

□ **B)** Shower

□ **C)** Drizzle

□ **D)** Spitting

3. In 1608, the first Frost Fair was held on the frozen River Thames. From then on, the freezing of the river brought carnivalesque celebrations to the city. When was the last London Frost Fair held?

□ **A)** 1800

□ **B)** 1814

□ **C)** 1856

□ **D)** 1890

4. Until November 2017, Sheffield held the global record for the longest-lasting rainbow. For how long was it visible on 14 March 1994?

 ☐ **A)** 8 hours

 ☐ **B)** 10 hours

 ☐ **C)** 3 hours

 ☐ **D)** 6 hours

5. BBC Radio 4's Shipping Forecast is beloved by mariners and insomniacs alike. But what controversial change was made in 2002?

 ☐ **A)** The name of a sea area was changed

 ☐ **B)** It introduced new theme music

 ☐ **C)** The broadcast was pushed back twelve minutes

 ☐ **D)** It stopped airing at all

6. Which of the following is NOT cockney rhyming slang for weather conditions?

 ☐ **A)** Taters in the mould

 ☐ **B)** Auntie Ella

 ☐ **C)** Turin Shroud

 ☐ **D)** Watch and chain

7. He had one job . . . Which BBC weather presenter became infamous for failing to flag what would go down in history as the Great Storm of 1987?

 ☐ **A)** Jim Bacon

 ☐ **B)** Jay Wynne

 ☐ **C)** Michael Fish

 ☐ **D)** Peter Cockroft

8. What bizarre event was recorded in 1830 over the Scottish Hebrides, and again in 1859 over South Wales?

    ☐ **A)** Fish fell from the sky

    ☐ **B)** A plague of locusts

    ☐ **C)** Acid rain

    ☐ **D)** A highly localized tornado

9. When did the Met Office start televising weather broadcasts, with a forecaster standing before a map?

    ☐ **A)** 1934

    ☐ **B)** 1944

    ☐ **C)** 1954

    ☐ **D)** 1964

10. It's a girl! And it's hitting north-west Scotland! What, in 2015, did the Met Office officially name its first storm?

    ☐ **A)** Aileen

    ☐ **B)** Abigail

    ☐ **C)** Andrea

    ☐ **D)** Aoife

11. According to English folklore, what happens if rain falls on St Swithin's Day, 15 July?

    ☐ **A)** More rain (for forty days)

    ☐ **B)** No rain until the autumnal equinox

    ☐ **C)** A dry winter

    ☐ **D)** A white Christmas

12. Since records began in 1922, how many Wimbledon champion-ships have been recorded WITHOUT interruptions for rain?

☐ **A)** 4

☐ **B)** 5

☐ **C)** 10

☐ **D)** 8

13. The 1976 drought remains one of the most severe on record, with a high recorded of 35.9 degrees Celsius. But how long did it last?

☐ **A)** 16 days

☐ **B)** 66 days

☐ **C)** 6 weeks

☐ **D)** 16 months

14. The Great Storm of 1703 was arguably the worst storm in Brit-ain's history. The Royal Navy lost 13 ships, every one of London's 120 church steeples was damaged, and a total of 8,000 people were killed. How did the government at the time respond?

☐ **A)** Banned storms

☐ **B)** Held a day of fasting

☐ **C)** Introduced a gale warning service

☐ **D)** Held a court of inquiry

15. Britain's highest mountain, Ben Nevis, recorded no snow for the first time in more than a decade, in what year?

☐ **A)** 2017

☐ **B)** 2021

☐ **C)** 2007

☐ **D)** 2002

16. What catchphrase was popularized by nineties skit comedy *The Fast Show*?

 ☐ **A)** 'I burn before I tan.'

 ☐ **B)** 'Blazing.'

 ☐ **C)** 'Scorchio!'

 ☐ **D)** 'It's hotter than the sun out there.'

17. What's the significance, in forecasting, of 'the 528 line'?

 ☐ **A)** Sunshine hours

 ☐ **B)** Air temperature

 ☐ **C)** Air density

 ☐ **D)** Possible snow

18. Which of the below receives the most average rainfall annually?

 ☐ **A)** Scotland

 ☐ **B)** Wales

 ☐ **C)** England

 ☐ **D)** Ireland

19. Which of the below is NOT a kind of frost?

 ☐ **A)** Hoar

 ☐ **B)** Glaze

 ☐ **C)** Rime

 ☐ **D)** Blinter

20. What is the name of the mathematical formula used to determine the winner of a cricket match, should rain stop play?

☐ **A)** Duckworth-Lewis-Stern

☐ **B)** Irwin-Wakefield-Walker

☐ **C)** Tawn-Thatcher-Graunt

☐ **D)** Hibbert-Heysham-Haines

21. Which delicious dessert lends its name to the cold winds prevalent on the north-eastern coasts of England?

☐ **A)** Trifle breeze

☐ **B)** Custard winds

☐ **C)** Crumble gale

☐ **D)** Ice-cream showers

22. What weather event is sometimes called a 'cow-quaker'?

☐ **A)** A recurring breeze in the Hebrides

☐ **B)** Wind speeds of over 40mph

☐ **C)** A storm in May

☐ **D)** Unexpected snowfall overnight

23. The deepest snow ever recorded in an inhabited area of the UK was in the winter of 1946–7 – but where?

☐ **A)** Durham

☐ **B)** Glasgow

☐ **C)** Kent

☐ **D)** Wales

24. Which of the below is the specification for 'storm', wind force 10 on the twelve-point Beaufort Scale?

- ☐ **A)** 'Twigs break off trees, generally impedes progress. Wave crests begin to break into spindrift.'
- ☐ **B)** 'Whole trees in motion; inconvenience felt when walking against the wind. Foam blown in streaks across the sea.'
- ☐ **C)** 'Very rarely experienced, accompanied by widespread damage. Medium-sized ships lost to view behind waves. Sea covered in white foam, visibility seriously affected.'
- ☐ **D)** 'Trees uprooted; considerable structural damage; sea surface is largely white.'

25. Even during the conquest of England, we were thinking about the weather. The Bayeux Tapestry of the 1070s depicts a man installing a rooster weathervane on which building?

- ☐ **A)** Westminster Abbey
- ☐ **B)** Norwich Cathedral
- ☐ **C)** Durham Castle
- ☐ **D)** Shrewsbury Abbey

A. 188

2. Food and Drink

You're expecting to read something sneering here, aren't you? Some schoolyard gags about jellied eels and spotted dick, warm pints and round-the-clock tea-drinking, bland Britain or great big pile of flavourless carbs. But we're not going to dignify that discourse.

Yes, British food has a globe-spanning, time-honoured reputation for being – shall we say – below average. Yes, it's probably fair to say that, left to their own devices – without the spoils of empire and lessons of multiculturalism – it may never have occurred to the Anglo Saxons to season a chicken breast. And yes, it's a fact white pudding is a thing.

But every couple of months, with grimly predictable regularity, some American news outlet will publish an article with a headline like 'Fourteen Awful British Foods That Make Us Feel Proud to be American', or 'Why British Food is Terrible', and 'Sixteen British Foods That I, a Brit, Can't Believe People Actually Eat', and it's about time the record was corrected.

Britain also thought to pair sausages with mashed potatoes, and battered fish with fried potatoes, and to put crisps between slices of bread. It gave the world chicken tikka masala, and the sandwich, and the sausage roll. In Britain, you don't even have to mush your peas yourself: you can buy them that way!

And then there's the full English: as effective a cure for what ails you as penicillin (also a British invention). Surely we can look past any amount of wallpaper-paste-like bread sauce or tasteless blanched vegetables for that. Even black pudding has a lot to recommend it.

More to the point, Britain has got over its historic hesitancy to experiment with flavour and 'foodie culture' and now ranks among the world's best in terms of cuisine. When the first edition of France's *Michelin Guide* was launched in 1974, just twenty-five stars in total were awarded to British and Irish restaurants. By 2011, that was up to more than 143 establishments.

So what's behind the American press's ongoing fixation with 'bad British food'? You might say, if you were feeling provocative, that America is insecure about its status as a fading world superpower and deprived because of chocolate that tastes weirdly grainy and ashy, like you've just taken a big mouthful out of your doormat.

But the most important thing is: no one is allowed to make fun of British food, except for us Brits. After all, we're the ones who have to eat it.

A. 192

Questions

1. What does the 'HP' stand for in 'HP sauce'?

- ☐ **A)** Heinz Product
- ☐ **B)** Harry Potter
- ☐ **C)** Houses of Parliament
- ☐ **D)** Henry Price

2. In setting a cake stand for afternoon tea, which item would traditionally be presented on the top tier?

- ☐ **A)** Butter
- ☐ **B)** Sandwiches
- ☐ **C)** Pastries
- ☐ **D)** Scones

3. Which of these iconic British companies is NOT actually British?

- ☐ **A)** Heinz
- ☐ **B)** Twinings
- ☐ **C)** Mr Kipling
- ☐ **D)** Cadbury

4. What does the 'PG' in 'PG Tips' stand for?

- ☐ **A)** Parental Guidance
- ☐ **B)** Pre-Gest
- ☐ **C)** Pungent Grey
- ☐ **D)** Post-Grain

5. What unlikely inclusion is often found inside a 'Sussex pond pudding'?

    ☐ **A)** A whole lemon

    ☐ **B)** A silver coin

    ☐ **C)** A button

    ☐ **D)** A loaf of bread

6. In a miraculous stand against inflation, the price of a portion of a minimum of ten strawberries and cream at Wimbledon has been steady since 2010. What is it?

    ☐ **A)** £3.50

    ☐ **B)** £1.70

    ☐ **C)** £2.50

    ☐ **D)** £4.20

7. Paddington Bear famously loves marmalade sandwiches. But what impact did the 2017 release of *Paddington 2* have on the fortunes of the spread?

    ☐ **A)** Prompted the inaugural World Marmalade Awards and Festival

    ☐ **B)** Increased sales after a steady decline

    ☐ **C)** Sparked a row among producers about inaccurate depiction

    ☐ **D)** Forced a change to the Wilkin & Sons recipe

8. Scotch eggs combine a boiled egg, sausage meat and bread-crumbs, to be baked or deep-fried – allegedly as a convenient travelling snack for the well-heeled. But what were the eighteenth-century eggs originally covered in, in place of sausage?

- ☐ **A)** Fish paste
- ☐ **B)** Stuffing
- ☐ **C)** Raisins
- ☐ **D)** Mushy peas

9. Which of the below was NOT a recipe of Britain's first celebrity chef, Fanny Cradock?

- ☐ **A)** Cygnet roasted
- ☐ **B)** Squirrel casserole
- ☐ **C)** Rose petal jam
- ☐ **D)** Baked hedgehog

10. The 'Black Velvet' combines Guinness with what?

- ☐ **A)** Milk
- ☐ **B)** Champagne
- ☐ **C)** Lemonade
- ☐ **D)** Coffee liqueur

11. The Bisto brand produces flavoured gravy powders, granules and sauces. But what does BISTO stand for, back to its origin in the early twentieth century?

- ☐ **A)** Browning Instant Stock Thickener in One
- ☐ **B)** Best In Supermarket Taste Options
- ☐ **C)** Believe In Saving Time Off
- ☐ **D)** Browns Instantly, Seasons and Thickens in One

12. Angel Delight was a popular powdered dessert throughout the 1970s, then its popularity waned. Which British icons were enlisted to boost its popularity in the 1990s?

    ☐ **A)** Wallace and Gromit

    ☐ **B)** The Wombles

    ☐ **C)** Basil Brush

    ☐ **D)** All of the above

13. How many sandwiches do Britons buy every year, to the closest billion?

    ☐ **A)** 4 billion

    ☐ **B)** 1 billion

    ☐ **C)** 3 billion

    ☐ **D)** 5 billion

14. Coronation chicken, a recipe created for Queen Elizabeth II's coronation, makes use of a highly original combination of ingredients. Which of the below is NOT included in the original 1953 recipe?

    ☐ **A)** Mayonnaise

    ☐ **B)** Dried apricots

    ☐ **C)** Curry powder

    ☐ **D)** Sultanas

15. Which Brit is credited with inventing chocolate?

    ☐ **A)** Joseph Fry

    ☐ **B)** John Cadbury

    ☐ **C)** Joseph William Thornton

    ☐ **D)** Henry Isaac Rowntree

16. In February 2023, a 32-year-old man was accused of stealing £31,000 worth of what food item?

    ☐ **A)** Baby formula

    ☐ **B)** Hard cheeses

    ☐ **C)** Easter eggs

    ☐ **D)** Shellfish

17. Under what name were Monster Munch crisps originally launched in 1977?

    ☐ **A)** Monster Mash

    ☐ **B)** Big Munchers

    ☐ **C)** Big Foots

    ☐ **D)** Prime Monster

18. What is the distinguishing feature of the 'stargazy pie'?

    ☐ **A)** A ceramic bird pie

    ☐ **B)** Fish heads

    ☐ **C)** Served with a fried egg

    ☐ **D)** Pineapple slice on top

19. Which of the below is NOT a regional term for bread within Great Britain?

    ☐ **A)** Cob

    ☐ **B)** Bara

    ☐ **C)** Stotty

    ☐ **D)** Stovie

20. What kind of food is mulligatawny, first described in an 1818 cookbook?

    ☐ **A)** Stew

    ☐ **B)** Soup

    ☐ **C)** Spice

    ☐ **D)** A root vegetable

21. Chicken tikka masala was hailed by the late foreign minister Robin Cook as 'a true British national dish'. In which city was it invented?

    ☐ **A)** Glasgow

    ☐ **B)** Reading

    ☐ **C)** Leicester

    ☐ **D)** Birmingham

22. What distinguishes a shepherd's pie from a cottage pie or a Cumberland pie?

    ☐ **A)** Where they are made

    ☐ **B)** Different meats

    ☐ **C)** Different herbs and flavourings

    ☐ **D)** Preparation of the potatoes

23. What is the record for the most pubs visited by an individual in twenty-four hours?

    ☐ **A)** 24

    ☐ **B)** 44

    ☐ **C)** 51

    ☐ **D)** 73

24. Which drink is NOT featured in Chumbawamba's 1997 anthem 'Tubthumping?'

- ☐ **A)** Fizzy drink
- ☐ **B)** Vodka
- ☐ **C)** Cider
- ☐ **D)** Lager

25. What is added to Welsh rarebit to make buck rarebit?

- ☐ **A)** Ham
- ☐ **B)** Egg
- ☐ **C)** Mustard
- ☐ **D)** Parsley

A. 192

3. History

The one thing you can say of British history: there's certainly a lot of it. Though, at school, while we may seem to focus on Henry VIII's many wives and their untimely deaths, the Tudors are just one chapter in a story that goes back hundreds of thousands of years (albeit one that makes the brutal competition for mates on *Love Island* seem civilized).

Stone tools discovered by archaeologists in Norfolk in the early twenty-first century suggest the presence of humans in Britain between 800,000 and 1 million years ago. Just to give you a reference point, the Roman conquest of Britain was begun by emperor Claudius in AD 43. And this year is . . . you don't really need us to tell you that, do you?

The point is, as much British history has been recorded, in books and censuses and multipart television documentaries hosted by Tony Robinson, there is even more that we have never known – and may never find out. Our picture of Britain's ancient history is dependent on what we can glean from archaeological research: obviously an image that is lacking in detail.

As we duly commit to memory the names of Henry's wives, or the British sovereigns in order of their reigns, or the start and end dates of all the wars as proof of our engagement with these islands' long and illustrious past, we might do well to remember that these pictures are incomplete too.

History has always been recorded from a particular perspective – mostly that of educated men whose focus has overwhelmingly been on other men, their wars and empires. Many experiences of the past have been lost, even as people are now working hard to uncover them.

For instance, Black people have been part of British society since Roman times: 'Beachy Head Lady', a woman from sub-Saharan Africa whose remains were found in East Sussex, grew up in a quintessentially English village 1,700 years ago. Yet mainstream historical understanding has focused on the Windrush generation of immigrants who arrived in the mid-twentieth century.

Even that has been publicized only relatively recently, as part of a renewed push to recognize that Britain has never been a monoculture. Nor has it always been 'Great' for everyone – as the ongoing reckoning over the legacy of the British empire goes to show.

The point is, not only is there a vast amount of British history as it's written, it is being rewritten all the time as we make new dis-coveries, revisit historic accounts and reckon with what we might have got wrong – or missed entirely.

Sure, it's a lot to consider, and properly impossible to learn by heart – but making the effort to understand, rather than merely memorize, makes the already long, dramatic, bloody and fascinat-ing British history even richer.

In the meantime, here's a bit of trivia. (Answers correct at time of writing.)

A. 195

Questions

1. Who or what was the origin of the now-ubiquitous expression of Britishness 'Keep calm and carry on'?
- ☐ **A)** King George VI
- ☐ **B)** Winston Churchill
- ☐ **C)** Lord Herbert Kitchener
- ☐ **D)** The government

2. Florence Nightingale was well known as a 'ministering angel' during the Crimean War. As well as nursing, how else did she make an impact on the world?
- ☐ **A)** Statistician
- ☐ **B)** Caterer
- ☐ **C)** Sanitary inspector
- ☐ **D)** Seamstress

3. Before settling on the WorldWideWeb, Tim Berners-Lee considered other names for his invention. Which one of the below was NOT in the mix?
- ☐ **A)** Information Mesh
- ☐ **B)** The Information Mine
- ☐ **C)** The International Web
- ☐ **D)** Mine of Information

4. 1666 was deemed 'Annus Mirabilis', the year of miracles, by poet John Dryden – despite being marked by great tragedy. Which catastrophic event defined that September?

☐ **A)** The Second Anglo-Dutch War

☐ **B)** The Great Fire of London

☐ **C)** The Great Plague

☐ **D)** The most intense tornado on record

5. Of all the wars that England has fought, at home and abroad, which killed the highest proportion of English soldiers?

☐ **A)** The English Civil War

☐ **B)** The First World War

☐ **C)** The Falklands War

☐ **D)** The Boer War

6. Which raid in AD 793 was said to usher in the 'Viking age'?

☐ **A)** Fulford

☐ **B)** Carhampton

☐ **C)** Edington

☐ **D)** Lindisfarne

7. Remember, remember, the fifth of November. Which monarch was the target of the Gunpowder Plot of 1605?

☐ **A)** James I

☐ **B)** Edward II

☐ **C)** Charles II

☐ **D)** Henry V

8. Sylvia Beckingham played an important part in the history of the NHS: what was it?

    ☐ **A)** Founder of the NHS

    ☐ **B)** First woman doctor

    ☐ **C)** First patient

    ☐ **D)** First mother to give birth on the NHS

9. After the Aberfan disaster of 1966, when 150,000 tonnes of coal waste collapsed into the Welsh village killing 116 children, who was ordered to pay for the remaining coal tips to be removed?

    ☐ **A)** The residents of Aberfan

    ☐ **B)** The National Coal Board

    ☐ **C)** The Welsh government

    ☐ **D)** The coal company

10. What is Scottish inventor James Watt's best-known achievement, often credited with beginning the Industrial Revolution?

    ☐ **A)** Improving production of cloth with the spinning jenny

    ☐ **B)** Developing the steam engine

    ☐ **C)** Inventing the steam engine

    ☐ **D)** Inventing the locomotive engine

11. What is the oldest manufacturing company in Britain, dating back to 1570?

    ☐ **A)** Firmin & Sons

    ☐ **B)** The Whitechapel Bell Foundry

    ☐ **C)** Robert Noble

    ☐ **D)** Castrol

12. What was the Nazi codename for a planned invasion of Britain during the Second World War?

☐ **A)** Sea Lion

☐ **B)** Case White

☐ **C)** Birke

☐ **D)** Büffel

13. Between 1700 to 1900 there was a shift from living in villages to living in towns and cities for work. Of the below, which had the biggest population at the 1801 census?

☐ **A)** Bristol

☐ **B)** Liverpool

☐ **C)** Birmingham

☐ **D)** Manchester

14. Which document did many adult Scottish males sign in 1638, committing themselves to defending the 'true Church' of Scotland against reforms proposed by King Charles I?

☐ **A)** Beggars' Summons

☐ **B)** Negative Confession

☐ **C)** Claim of Right

☐ **D)** National Covenant

15. The name England originates from the Old English name 'Engla-land', meaning . . . what?

☐ **A)** Land of the Angles

☐ **B)** Even (as in flat) land

☐ **C)** Even (as in fair) land

☐ **D)** Angel-land

16. What was an official language of England for nearly three hundred years?

- ☐ **A)** Dutch
- ☐ **B)** German
- ☐ **C)** French
- ☐ **D)** Welsh

17. Of the new polymer Ulster Bank notes, only the £50 note displays a particular person. Who is it?

- ☐ **A)** Footballer George Best
- ☐ **B)** Actor Kenneth Branagh
- ☐ **C)** Astrophysicist Jocelyn Bell-Burnell
- ☐ **D)** Choreographer Helen Lewis

18. The 1916 Easter Rising began in Dublin on which day?

- ☐ **A)** Easter Monday
- ☐ **B)** Easter Sunday
- ☐ **C)** Good Friday
- ☐ **D)** Shrove Tuesday

19. Who were the Edinburgh Seven, who made headlines in 1869?

- ☐ **A)** Scotland's first Labour MPs
- ☐ **B)** Leaders within the trade-union movement
- ☐ **C)** A notorious band of grave-robbers, or 'resurrection men'
- ☐ **D)** The first women to matriculate at a British university

20. What was the only item that Shakespeare specified should be left to his wife, Anne Hathaway, in his will?

☐ **A)** Their 'second-best bed'

☐ **B)** His gold signet ring

☐ **C)** His 'night stool', for evening ablutions

☐ **D)** His 'money box'

21. The Great Domesday Book (the largest volume of the Domesday survey, prepared for William the Conquerer) mentions 16,667 individual men. How many women does it mention?

☐ **A)** 12,045

☐ **B)** None

☐ **C)** 479

☐ **D)** Only Matilda of Flanders

22. What kind of plague was the Black Death?

☐ **A)** Bubonic plague

☐ **B)** Pneumonic plague

☐ **C)** Septicaemic plague

☐ **D)** All three

23. In the Wars of the Roses, Queen Margaret of Anjou was the Lancasters' most skilled strategist. Who did she enlist to decide upon the execution of two Yorkists?

☐ **A)** Her young son

☐ **B)** Their wives

☐ **C)** Her former husband

☐ **D)** Edward IV

24. What was the name of Napoleon's favourite war horse at the Battle of Waterloo?

- ☐ **A)** Ajax
- ☐ **B)** Marengo
- ☐ **C)** Achilles
- ☐ **D)** Comanche

25. The Anglo-Zanzibar War of 1896 is considered the shortest war in history. How long did it last?

- ☐ **A)** 45 days
- ☐ **B)** 5 days
- ☐ **C)** 45 minutes
- ☐ **D)** 40 weeks

A. 195

4. Football

When it comes to questions of Britishness, it doesn't matter whether you yourself follow football or not: it is without a doubt part of life. With football fans not only the most visible of all sports supporters in the UK, but also arguably the most patriotic, what we conceive of as 'England' in particular has been shaped in their image.

Consider the unofficial national anthem 'Three Lions', recorded by comedy duo David Baddiel and Frank Skinner and the rock band The Lightning Seeds for the 1996 Euros and regularly recirculated since. With its chorus of 'It's coming home', laying a claim on the entire sport as belonging to England, it's often seen to be triumphant, even cocksure – not least by the English team's opponents on the pitch, who have often criticized the fans' chant as arrogant and entitled.

But Baddiel and Skinner have said that the song was meant to be tongue-in-cheek, expressing the hope, even self-delusion, that keeps fans from despair after yet another loss. 'Unless you're a fan of *Fawlty Towers* and stuff like that, maybe you don't get the slant on it,' said England manager Gareth Southgate in 2018.

Of course, football fans haven't always been known for their good humour, especially in the face of defeat. Football hooliganism was once so widespread a problem that it was known as 'the English disease'. Both the sport and the bad behaviour dates back to the Middle Ages, with football matches little more than organized fights between the young men of rival villages and towns.

According to the anthropologist Kate Fox, only two brief periods in British history were fleetingly free of football-related violence: the interwar years, and about a ten-year period after the Second World War.

Organized (and often racialized) violence peaked in the 1970s and 1980s, prompting a concerted clampdown by police. By the early 1990s, most grounds were considered safe destinations, and fans of opposing teams could even be counted on to travel alongside each other without incident.

Still, past upheaval has cast a long shadow. Even into the 2000s, football hooliganism was a recurring and contentious point in discussions of the UK's national identity and often singled out as a defining characteristic.

But lately – while there are still occasional outbreaks of unruliness among fans – the English football team has come to represent the best of us. Under Gareth Southgate the national side is widely seen to have led the sport on issues of diversity and inclusion.

In an open letter published in the UK national press Southgate directly addressed 'dear England': 'we have a desire to protect our values and traditions, as we should, but that shouldn't come at the expense of introspection or progress'.

Off the pitch, too, captain Harry Kane and players Marcus Rashford and Raheem Stirling have publicly stood up for action against child poverty and racist abuse, even when it has meant defying their fans, sporting bodies and the UK government.

Plus: they have played good football. In 2021, England reached its first major-tournament final since 1966, and with its most diverse squad ever. As rappers Dave and Stormzy put it in a television spot ahead of the Euros final: 'The past can't hurt us. The future can inspire us. This is England – modern England.'

A. 199

Questions

1. Who played England in the world's first ever international football match in 1872?

- ☐ **A)** Germany
- ☐ **B)** France
- ☐ **C)** Spain
- ☐ **D)** Scotland

2. Which British team was the first to win the European Cup/ Champions League?

- ☐ **A)** Celtic
- ☐ **B)** Leeds United
- ☐ **C)** Liverpool
- ☐ **D)** Manchester United

3. Which footballer was famously declared 'daft as a brush' by his one-time manager?

- ☐ **A)** David Beckham
- ☐ **B)** Paul Gascoigne
- ☐ **C)** Wayne Rooney
- ☐ **D)** Sol Campbell

4. England won the Women's Euro 2022 final against Germany. But who did they beat in the semis?

- ☐ **A)** Sweden
- ☐ **B)** Spain
- ☐ **C)** Italy
- ☐ **D)** France

5. Manchester United's hallowed home ground is well known as 'The Theatre of Dreams'. But who came up with the name?

- ☐ **A)** George Best
- ☐ **B)** Sir Alex Ferguson
- ☐ **C)** Sir Bobby Charlton
- ☐ **D)** Writer John Riley

6. Who scored the first 'perfect hat-trick' (left foot, right foot and header) in the Premier League?

- ☐ **A)** Jimmy Floyd Hasselbaink
- ☐ **B)** Peter Crouch
- ☐ **C)** Eric Cantona
- ☐ **D)** Mark Robins

7. Why is King Edward III believed to have banned medieval football in 1363?

- ☐ **A)** The first pitch invasion
- ☐ **B)** To shut down emerging friendly relations with France
- ☐ **C)** Complaints of noise and disruptive crowds
- ☐ **D)** To boost archery

8. The 'Royal Shrovetide Football' game of medieval football, or 'hugball', is played annually on Shrove Tuesday and Ash Wednesday in the Derbyshire town of Ashbourne. Which of the below is NOT a rule still observed today?

- ☐ **A)** No more than six players to a side
- ☐ **B)** No carrying the ball in a motorized vehicle
- ☐ **C)** No committing murder or manslaughter
- ☐ **D)** No playing after 10 p.m.

9. The crowd noise heard at the beginning of Baddiel and Skinner's Euro '96 anthem 'Three Lions' is sampled from which game?

- ☐ **A)** Ipswich v Manchester United in 1995
- ☐ **B)** The Euro '94 final between Germany and the Czech Republic
- ☐ **C)** A League Cup game between Chelsea and West Bromwich Albion in 1993
- ☐ **D)** A UEFA Cup game between Liverpool and Danish side Brondby

10. What colour was Manchester United's kit before they adopted red and white?

- ☐ **A)** Blue
- ☐ **B)** Green and white
- ☐ **C)** Green and gold
- ☐ **D)** Black and white

11. Geoff Hurst scored a hat-trick in the 1966 FIFA World Cup final victory over West Germany. But who scored England's other goal?

☐ **A)** Bobby Moore

☐ **B)** Martin Peters

☐ **C)** Ray Wilson

☐ **D)** Alan Ball

12. Who was José Mourinho speaking about when he famously said: 'I'm not going to lose my hair to speak about X'?

☐ **A)** Pep Guardiola

☐ **B)** Zinedine Zidane

☐ **C)** Luciano Spalletti

☐ **D)** Antonio Conte

13. Why was Mourinho arrested and cautioned for obstruction in May 2007?

☐ **A)** Alleged assault of a player

☐ **B)** Resisting quarantine of his pet dog

☐ **C)** Derailing a press conference

☐ **D)** Public urination

14. With more than 170 caps to her name, which player has made the most appearances for the England women's national team?

☐ **A)** Fara Williams

☐ **B)** Jill Scott

☐ **C)** Karen Carney

☐ **D)** Casey Stoney

15. Who is the only player to win the Champions League with three different clubs?

- ☐ **A)** Samuel Eto'o
- ☐ **B)** Clarence Seedorf
- ☐ **C)** Xabi Alonso
- ☐ **D)** Jose Bosingwa

16. Which of these managers has never managed in the Premier League?

- ☐ **A)** Michael Laudrup
- ☐ **B)** Nigel Clough
- ☐ **C)** Carlos Carvalhal
- ☐ **D)** Jacques Santini

17. Which of the below is a real nickname for a Premier League or EFL team?

- ☐ **A)** The Albatrosses
- ☐ **B)** The Bluetits
- ☐ **C)** The Jays
- ☐ **D)** The Bluebirds

18. What name did Wales's New Saints FC go by between 1997 and 2006?

- ☐ **A)** BT
- ☐ **B)** Clwb Pêl-droed y Seintiau Newydd
- ☐ **C)** Total Network Solutions
- ☐ **D)** Llansantffraid

19. Formed in 1854, which club was the first English sports club to use the word 'United' in its name?

- ☐ **A)** Sheffield United
- ☐ **B)** Manchester United
- ☐ **C)** Newcastle United
- ☐ **D)** Oxford United

20. Alan Shearer is the Premier League's all-time leading goal scorer, but who has the record for assists?

- ☐ **A)** Cesc Fàbregas
- ☐ **B)** Ryan Giggs
- ☐ **C)** Kevin De Bruyne
- ☐ **D)** David Silva

21. Which team won the first ever FA Cup final in 1872?

- ☐ **A)** Wanderers FC
- ☐ **B)** Royal Engineers
- ☐ **C)** Harrow Chequers
- ☐ **D)** Reigate Priory

22. Which was the last Welsh team to compete in the English Premier League?

- ☐ **A)** Wrexham
- ☐ **B)** Swansea City
- ☐ **C)** Newport County
- ☐ **D)** Cardiff City

23. Peter Schmeichel was the first goalkeeper to score in the Premier League. Which club was he playing for at the time?

☐ **A)** Manchester United

☐ **B)** Manchester City

☐ **C)** Aston Villa

☐ **D)** Leicester City

24. Which British footballer is considered the first Black man to have played international football?

☐ **A)** Arthur Wharton

☐ **B)** Eddie Parris

☐ **C)** Viv Anderson

☐ **D)** Andrew Watson

25. Who is the top-scoring player in the Scottish Premier Football League?

☐ **A)** Kris Boyd

☐ **B)** Henrik Larsson

☐ **C)** Ally McCoist

☐ **D)** Scott McDonald

A. 199

5. Sport

Over hundreds of thousands of years of British history there has never been a time when sport wasn't of central importance – at least as central as food, say, or politics. Many people would say more so.

The Celtic tribes engaged in running, wrestling and ball games. Later, the Romans raised the stakes with chariot racing and gladiatorial contests, often meeting with a gruesome end. Medieval Britain saw the emergence of archery and jousting. And if you think sport is any less central to our national identity now, ask anyone who was in London in 2012 about the Summer Olympics and watch their eyes mist over. You'd swear that it was the last time they felt joy.

Likewise, go to any pub and notice the number of diversions: darts, billiards, quiz machines, even a crumbling box of Scrabble in the corner. Heaven forbid that you actually have to talk to each other.

There's something about competition that unites Britons, even as it ostensibly pits us against each other. Perhaps sport and games present us with a route back to our schooldays, granting us a socially permissible, structured outlet for our innate competitiveness and desire to play.

Even if you were to set aside football as the pre-eminent national obsession, that still leaves you with athletics, boxing, rugby, cricket, cycling, tennis, golf, motorsports and horseracing to keep you occupied. Follow enough sports and you might not have time or headspace to pay attention to anything else. (Perhaps that's the point?)

Either way, it seems no coincidence that nearly every sport or game still popular today has its roots in Britain. Good sportsmanship, even in defeat, is considered a national value – though, as is often the case with our positive attributes, it has a dark past.

In the days of the British empire, sport was used as a means of spreading and enforcing imperial rule. Setting aside claims that cricket originated in India and was another spoil of empire, the so-called 'gentleman's game' was certainly one way in which British standards of behaviour and moral codes were imposed.

Indeed, the way the British empire deployed sports, games and all their associated rules is not unlike how it made use of religion with its Christian missionaries: equal part to the empire's 'civilizing' mission in the colonies.

These days, however, sport is perhaps one of the ways Britons most readily come together on a relatively even playing field in a highly unequal society – just look at the unifying, multicultural, positive patriotism modelled by England's national side in the 2021 Euros.

Sport might not be the actual Church of England, but it can certainly be just as potent a force for moral instruction: an enjoyable, engrossing and occasionally edifying way to spend a Sunday afternoon.

A. 202

Questions

1. The longest ever match at Wimbledon used 123 balls – but how long did it last, to the closest hour?

    ☐ **A)** 8 hours

    ☐ **B)** 9 hours

    ☐ **C)** 11 hours

    ☐ **D)** 12 hours

2. The British Open golf tournament dates back to 1860. Which British player has won the most championship titles?

    ☐ **A)** Harry Vardon

    ☐ **B)** John Henry Taylor

    ☐ **C)** James Braid

    ☐ **D)** 'Old' Tom Morris

3. Who or what in 2016 cost Briton Alistair Brownlee first place in the men's elite category of the World Triathlon series in Mexico?

    ☐ **A)** His younger brother

    ☐ **B)** An injury

    ☐ **C)** Climate protesters

    ☐ **D)** A dog on the track

4. Who is the most successful British Formula One driver ever?

☐ **A)** Jim Clark

☐ **B)** Nigel Mansell

☐ **C)** Jackie Stewart

☐ **D)** Lewis Hamilton

5. In February 2023, 16-year-old Mia Brookes, from Cheshire, became the youngest world champion in the history of which sport?

☐ **A)** Archery

☐ **B)** Table tennis

☐ **C)** Snowboarding

☐ **D)** Skateboarding

6. What is the crafty side hustle of Olympic gold-winning swimmer Tom Daley?

☐ **A)** Handmade soaps

☐ **B)** Crochet

☐ **C)** Hot sauce

☐ **D)** Pottery

7. At which English cricket ground would you find the Nursery End?

☐ **A)** The Oval

☐ **B)** Old Trafford

☐ **C)** Trent Bridge

☐ **D)** Lord's

8. Which batsman has scored the highest aggregate of runs in first-class cricket?

    ☐ **A)** Jack Hobbs

    ☐ **B)** W. G. Grace

    ☐ **C)** Don Bradman

    ☐ **D)** Frank Woolley

9. The Calcutta Cup, for rugby's Six Nations championship, is awarded to the winner of which fixture?

    ☐ **A)** England v Ireland

    ☐ **B)** England v Scotland

    ☐ **C)** Ireland v Scotland

    ☐ **D)** Wales v Scotland

10. Which country did England famously upset in the semi-finals of the 1999 Rugby World Cup?

    ☐ **A)** New Zealand

    ☐ **B)** France

    ☐ **C)** South Africa

    ☐ **D)** Australia

11. Brothers Alan and Chris Old both represented England on the same day in the 1970s, but in different sports. Which?

    ☐ **A)** Football and squash

    ☐ **B)** Cricket and rugby union

    ☐ **C)** Cricket and football

    ☐ **D)** Sailing and badminton

12. Which unexpected athlete has NOT represented Britain at the Olympics?

- ☐ **A)** Darth Vader stunt double Bob Anderson
- ☐ **B)** Princess Anne
- ☐ **C)** Codebreaker Alan Turing
- ☐ **D)** Former Liberal Democrat party leader Menzies 'Ming' Campbell

13. In 2021 Jason Kenny became the most successful Olympic athlete in British history, with seven gold medals. What is his sport?

- ☐ **A)** Archery
- ☐ **B)** Cycling
- ☐ **C)** Sailing
- ☐ **D)** Fencing

14. In which city was the Commonwealth Games held in 2014?

- ☐ **A)** Glasgow
- ☐ **B)** Birmingham
- ☐ **C)** Manchester
- ☐ **D)** Edinburgh

15. The first World Snooker Championship was held in 1927. What did the 'Sultan of Snooker' Joe Davis take home for first prize?

- ☐ **A)** £500,000
- ☐ **B)** Nothing
- ☐ **C)** Land
- ☐ **D)** Change from a tenner

16. 25-year-old medical student Roger Bannister became the first person to break the four-minute mile in 1954. How long did his record last?

☐ **A)** 6 weeks

☐ **B)** 6 days

☐ **C)** 6 months

☐ **D)** 6 years

17. Which British player has the most caps in rugby history?

☐ **A)** Gethin Jenkins

☐ **B)** Brian O'Driscoll

☐ **C)** Alun Wyn Jones

☐ **D)** Ronan O'Gara

18. How many world titles has Phil 'the Power' Taylor won in darts?

☐ **A)** 12

☐ **B)** 9

☐ **C)** 16

☐ **D)** 7

19. What is the name of professional boxer Tyson Fury's brand of energy drink?

☐ **A)** Furocity

☐ **B)** Furyade

☐ **C)** Fighter

☐ **D)** Monster

20. Who did Andy Murray ultimately beat to win Olympic gold in Rio in 2016?

    ☐ **A)** Novak Djokovic

    ☐ **B)** Juan Martin del Potro

    ☐ **C)** Kei Nishikori

    ☐ **D)** Roger Federer

21. What is Becher's Brook?

    ☐ **A)** A hole at St Andrews' Old Course

    ☐ **B)** A stage of the Tour de France

    ☐ **C)** A trophy in rugby union

    ☐ **D)** A fence jumped in the Grand National

22. How was the inaugural Golden Globe round-the-world yacht race of 1968 derailed?

    ☐ **A)** A sailor faked his location

    ☐ **B)** A yacht struck a whale, forcing an emergency rescue

    ☐ **C)** Not a single sailor completed the circumnavigation

    ☐ **D)** The yacht in the lead was attacked by pirates

23. Which of the below is NOT a real-life term in cricket, much to the general merriment of overseas media?

    ☐ **A)** Dibbly-dobbler

    ☐ **B)** Googly

    ☐ **C)** Doosra

    ☐ **D)** Drooler

24. Wimbledon was not always the home of tennis. What was its focus when it was founded in 1868?

- ☐ **A)** Cricket
- ☐ **B)** Croquet
- ☐ **C)** Football
- ☐ **D)** Lawn bowls

25. In September 2021 Emma Raducanu became the first British woman to win a Grand Slam title since 1977. Who won it in that year?

- ☐ **A)** Virginia Wade
- ☐ **B)** Angela Mortimer
- ☐ **C)** Sue Barker
- ☐ **D)** Ann Haydon-Jones

4. 202

6. Music

On 7 February 1964 The Beatles arrived in New York to great fan-fare and hysterical crowds. It marked the start of what went down in history as the 'second British invasion', when the coolest bands and singers in the world were all British.

London's Carnaby Street became known as the white-hot centre of the Swinging Sixties, with The Rolling Stones, Petula Clark, The Yardbirds, The Who, The Kinks, Dusty Springfield, The Dave Clark Five and Manfred Mann all hailing from Greater London.

But the rest of their cohort were, conspicuously, from all over Britain: Birmingham (Steve Winwood and the Spencer Davis Group, The Moody Blues), Manchester (The Hollies, Herman's Hermits), Newcastle (Eric Burdon and the Animals), Belfast (Van Morrison with Them) and St Albans (The Zombies).

Britain may never have been quite so close to centre stage since then – but we've never drifted too far from it, either. The impact of nineties rave culture and Cool Britannia, channelling the Swinging London spirit, is still felt today, not least in the ongoing calls for Oasis to get back together. (It's not going to happen.)

Decades after the Spice Girls (gone but never forgotten), Britain is still minting record-breaking pop groups like One Direc-tion (the first act to debut at number 1 with its first three albums) and Little Mix, who, in 2021, celebrated a hundred weeks in the Top 100. Glastonbury is still the world's most famous festival and bounced back from a pandemic bigger than ever.

Brits like Ed Sheeran, Adele, Coldplay, Dua Lipa and Harry Styles are among the biggest contemporary acts in the world. Even Taylor Swift declared herself a London girl for a time.

Meanwhile, Stormzy, Dave, Jorja Smith, Jai Paul and Sault make music that industries, artists and scenes the world over take notice of. Countercultures might be less visible now our music listening and fandom has migrated online, but there's still a British beat heard around the world.

A. 206

Questions

1. Which British musician was named a fellow of the Ivors Academy for songwriters in recognition of an 'outstanding music catalogue' in May 2023?

    ☐ **A)** Sting

    ☐ **B)** Mick Hucknall

    ☐ **C)** Phil Collins

    ☐ **D)** Rod Stewart

2. Which 1950s Scottish singer was an early inspiration for The Beatles and a host of countercultural icons?

    ☐ **A)** Jackie Dennis

    ☐ **B)** Andy Stewart

    ☐ **C)** Lonnie Donegan

    ☐ **D)** Marie Lawrie

3. Which singer was the first artist to make the Top 5 of the UK album chart across eight consecutive decades?

    ☐ **A)** Tom Jones

    ☐ **B)** Paul McCartney

    ☐ **C)** Elton John

    ☐ **D)** Cliff Richard

4. Who, in 1925, became the first Black woman to be broadcast on BBC Radio?

    □ **A)** Evelyn Dove

    □ **B)** Ella Fitzgerald

    □ **C)** Shirley Bassey

    □ **D)** Winifred Atwell

5. William Blake wrote the poem 'Jerusalem', but who set it to music a hundred years later?

    □ **A)** William Cowper

    □ **B)** Hubert Parry

    □ **C)** Isaac Watts

    □ **D)** John Newton

6. What is the name of the composer credited with creating the James Bond sound?

    □ **A)** John Williams

    □ **B)** John Barry

    □ **C)** David Arnold

    □ **D)** Monty Norman

7. Which of the below does NOT feature on the album cover of Pink Floyd's *Animals*?

    □ **A)** Dog

    □ **B)** Pig

    □ **C)** Cow

    □ **D)** Sheep

8. What was voted the greatest piece of British classical music by Classic FM listeners in 2023?

☐ **A)** 'Nimrod' by Edward Elgar

☐ **B)** 'Jupiter' by Holst

☐ **C)** 'The Lark Ascending' by Vaughan Williams

☐ **D)** 'The Armed Man' by Karl Jenkins

9. The memorable theme tune of *Doctor Who* was the work of which pioneering British electronic musician?

☐ **A)** Brian Eno

☐ **B)** Tristram Cary

☐ **C)** Janet Beat

☐ **D)** Delia Derbyshire

10. Which 1983 song and video was blacklisted by the BBC and prompted an on-air tirade from Radio 1 DJ Mike Read?

☐ **A)** 'Relax' by Frankie Goes to Hollywood

☐ **B)** 'Smalltown Boy' by Bronski Beat

☐ **C)** 'Dear God' by XTC

☐ **D)** 'Suicide Solution' by Ozzy Osbourne

11. Which Black classical musician and composer was mentored by both Joseph Haydn and Ludwig van Beethoven?

☐ **A)** George Bridgetower

☐ **B)** Joseph Antonio Emidy

☐ **C)** Samuel Coleridge-Taylor

☐ **D)** Rudolph Dunbar

12. Which of these public figures appears in three separate places on the album artwork for *Sergeant Pepper's Lonely Hearts Club Band*?

- ☐ **A)** Lawrence of Arabia
- ☐ **B)** John Lennon
- ☐ **C)** Carl Jung
- ☐ **D)** Shirley Temple

13. Where did the Pet Shop Boys get their name?

- ☐ **A)** Their first gig was at a pet shop
- ☐ **B)** Their friends worked at a pet shop
- ☐ **C)** They were inspired by The Beach Boys' *Pet Sounds*
- ☐ **D)** They loved animals

14. Which south London rapper made headlines for calling prime minister Boris Johnson 'a real racist' while performing freestyle at the Brit Awards in 2020?

- ☐ **A)** J. Hus
- ☐ **B)** Dave
- ☐ **C)** Burna Boy
- ☐ **D)** Stormzy

15. Which British band started out under the name Starfish?

- ☐ **A)** Talking Heads
- ☐ **B)** Radiohead
- ☐ **C)** Coldplay
- ☐ **D)** Pulp

16. Stormzy's first full-length project was titled *168: The Mixtape*. What was the 168 a reference to?

- ☐ **A)** The address of his family home
- ☐ **B)** His date of birth
- ☐ **C)** The rate of knife crime in London
- ☐ **D)** The time he spent making it

17. He went by many names: Ziggy Stardust, Aladdin Sane, The Thin White Duke . . . but which of the below was NOT an alias of David Bowie?

- ☐ **A)** The Laughing Gnome
- ☐ **B)** Founder, The Society for the Prevention of Cruelty to Long-haired Men
- ☐ **C)** Halloween Jack
- ☐ **D)** The Blind Prophet

18. Which of these mathematical symbols is NOT the title of an Ed Sheeran album?

- ☐ **A)** $\times$
- ☐ **B)** $/$
- ☐ **C)** $=$
- ☐ **D)** $\div$

19. One Direction was formed on *The X-Factor* in 2010. But who was the guest judge that put the single contestants together and changed British pop history for ever?

- ☐ **A)** Natalie Imbruglia
- ☐ **B)** Geri Halliwell
- ☐ **C)** Nicole Scherzinger
- ☐ **D)** Pixie Lott

20. Which of these names were The Beatles NOT once known by?

☐ **A)** The Quarrymen

☐ **B)** The Silver Beetles

☐ **C)** Johnny and the Moondogs

☐ **D)** The Blues Boys

21. Amy Winehouse's song 'Me and Mr Jones' is about a particular person. But who?

☐ **A)** Rapper Nas

☐ **B)** Tom Jones

☐ **C)** Quincy Jones

☐ **D)** Grace Jones

22. Geri Halliwell bade the Spice Girls 'Viva Forever' in May 1998. But in December of which year did the group announce that it was going on 'indefinite hiatus'?

☐ **A)** 1998

☐ **B)** 1999

☐ **C)** 2000

☐ **D)** 2001

23. Fatboy Slim's 1998 hit 'The Rockafeller Skank' samples which popular Northern Soul track?

☐ **A)** The Tams, 'Hey Girl Don't Bother Me'

☐ **B)** Al Wilson, 'The Snake'

☐ **C)** The Just Brothers, 'Sliced Tomatoes'

☐ **D)** Frank Wilson, 'Do I Love You (Indeed I Do)'

24. What did punk-rocker Johnny Lydon of the Sex Pistols contro-versially promote in 2009?

☐ **A)** *Daily Mail*

☐ **B)** BP

☐ **C)** British Lamb

☐ **D)** Butter

25. Who is the only artist or group to have won the Mercury Music Prize twice?

☐ **A)** P. J. Harvey

☐ **B)** Suede

☐ **C)** James Blake

☐ **D)** Gorillaz

A. 206

7. Art and Fashion

From the corsets and crinolines of the Victorian era, to the Mods and rockers of Swinging London, to the Cool Britannia era of wearing anoraks to award shows and accessorizing with Union Jack flags, Britain has always had a strong visual identity, as instantly recognizable as any Nike swoosh or McDonald's golden arches.

That reflects a tradition that has evolved with the nation itself, taking in influences from Europe and further afield. In the sixteenth and seventeenth centuries artists like Hans Holbein the Younger and Nicholas Hilliard were inspired by work they saw being produced as part of the Italian Renaissance.

Later, the Romantics channelled imagination, spirituality and nature to respond to an increasingly industrialized world. In the Victorian and Edwardian eras, art was valued as a means of exploring the times.

More recently, from the twentieth century on, even as Britain's reputation as a global superpower has waned, it has never drifted far from the centre of art, fashion and culture. There seems to be something about our wet island nation's innate discomfort with self-expression that fosters specific areas of excellence, such as tailoring, portraiture and landfill indie.

Even the famed London street style can be broken down into tribes and subcultures: the Burberry plaid, the safety-pins and newspaper-print of punk, the Hunter wellies and short-shorts at Glastonbury. This, in fact, is central to Britain's ongoing artistic success: knowing when to follow the rules, and when to break them.

A. 209

Questions

1. Who designed the wedding dress of the royal formerly known as Kate Middleton?

    ☐ **A)** Victoria Beckham

    ☐ **B)** Marchesa

    ☐ **C)** Stella McCartney

    ☐ **D)** Alexander McQueen

2. Which of these animals has contemporary artist Damien Hirst NOT interred in a vat of formaldehyde?

    ☐ **A)** Sheep

    ☐ **B)** Shark

    ☐ **C)** Zebra

    ☐ **D)** Hedgehog

3. What statement-making item did Stormzy wear in his 2019 Glastonbury headlining set?

    ☐ **A)** A stab-proof vest bearing the Union Jack

    ☐ **B)** Crown jewels made from coal

    ☐ **C)** A bloodstained Burberry trench

    ☐ **D)** A leather kilt

4. Which artist is known for his long-running collaboration with Radiohead?

    ☐ **A)** Stanley Donwood

    ☐ **B)** Richard Scarry

    ☐ **C)** Quentin Blake

    ☐ **D)** Maurice Sendak

5. You never know when, or where, Kate Moss will pop up. In which of the below does the supermodel NOT feature?

    ☐ **A)** Elton John's music video for 'Something about the Way You Look Tonight'

    ☐ **B)** *Absolutely Fabulous: The Movie*

    ☐ **C)** *Zoolander*

    ☐ **D)** *Blackadder Back & Forth*

6. What was the symbol of Swinging London, known as 'the five point of 1963'?

    ☐ **A)** A minidress

    ☐ **B)** A haircut

    ☐ **C)** A man's dress shoe

    ☐ **D)** A graphic eyeliner style

7. What was the name of Banksy's short-lived amusement park, set up in 2015 in Weston-super-Mare?

    ☐ **A)** Tragic Kingdom

    ☐ **B)** Warp Park

    ☐ **C)** Dismaland

    ☐ **D)** Haunted Towers

8. Who in 2017 became the first Black editor-in-chief of *British Vogue*?

- ☐ **A)** André Leon Talley
- ☐ **B)** Naomi Campbell
- ☐ **C)** Edward Enninful
- ☐ **D)** Elaine Welteroth

9. In 1992 lifelong agitator Vivienne Westwood was awarded an OBE. What did she famously wear to Buckingham Palace to accept the honour?

- ☐ **A)** No underwear
- ☐ **B)** A fur coat
- ☐ **C)** An inverted cross, a symbol of Satanism
- ☐ **D)** A Sex Pistols T-shirt

10. What was Selfridges contracted to produce during the First World War?

- ☐ **A)** Army uniforms
- ☐ **B)** The French army's underwear
- ☐ **C)** Union Jack flags
- ☐ **D)** Stretchers

11. Who of the below artists has NOT won the Turner Prize?

- ☐ **A)** Anish Kapoor
- ☐ **B)** Grayson Perry
- ☐ **C)** Antony Gormley
- ☐ **D)** Tracey Emin

12. County Fermanagh is home to a world-renowned pottery. What is it called?

- ☐ **A)** Belleek
- ☐ **B)** Leach pottery
- ☐ **C)** Carlton Ware
- ☐ **D)** Beswick

13. Which twentieth-century British sculptor died in a fire at her home?

- ☐ **A)** Phyllida Barlow
- ☐ **B)** Barbara Hepworth
- ☐ **C)** Elizabeth Frink
- ☐ **D)** Gertrude Hermes

14. Why was Damien Hirst's *Butterfly Bike*, once the world's most expensive bike, so named?

- ☐ **A)** Its feather-light weight
- ☐ **B)** The frame was built to resemble a butterfly
- ☐ **C)** It was covered with real butterfly wings
- ☐ **D)** Its uniquely impractical handlebar design

15. Henry Tate, a nineteenth-century merchant from Liverpool, was founding patron to the Tate Galleries. What product of his is still stocked in supermarkets?

- ☐ **A)** Cocoa powder
- ☐ **B)** Worcestershire sauce
- ☐ **C)** Jam
- ☐ **D)** Sugar cubes

16. Which leading portrait painter in eighteenth-century England created the masterpiece *The Blue Boy*, which was recently returned to the National Gallery?

☐ **A)** Thomas Gainsborough

☐ **B)** Sir Joshua Reynolds

☐ **C)** James Northcote

☐ **D)** Richard Wilson

17. Which of the below has NOT been the subject of a musical, for some (peculiarly British) reason?

☐ **A)** The Shoreditch Cereal Café

☐ **B)** Brexit

☐ **C)** The Great Plague of London

☐ **D)** The 2001 foot-and-mouth crisis

18. Which London theatre has the largest capacity?

☐ **A)** Apollo Victoria

☐ **B)** London Coliseum

☐ **C)** London Palladium

☐ **D)** Victoria Palace

19. It's a rite of passage for a British actor to play Hamlet – Kenneth Branagh has done it more than once, on stage and on screen. But who did he direct in the role in 2017?

☐ **A)** Christopher Eccleston

☐ **B)** Tom Hiddleston

☐ **C)** David Tennant

☐ **D)** Jude Law

20. Which English 'painter of light' is the first and only artist to grace a United Kingdom banknote?

□ **A)** William Blake

□ **B)** J. M. W. Turner

□ **C)** John Constable

□ **D)** John Martin

21. Which of the below is NOT an area of Tate Modern?

□ **A)** Natalie Bell Building

□ **B)** Blavatnik Building

□ **C)** Clore Studio

□ **D)** Turbine Hall

22. Which British painter, known for her optical-illusion-inspired artworks, was the first woman to win the International Prize for Painting at the Venice Biennale?

□ **A)** Lilian Andrews

□ **B)** Pauline Boty

□ **C)** Bridget Riley

□ **D)** Jann Haworth

23. Who was the first Black British woman to have her work enter the permanent collection of the Tate and to be elected to the prestigious Royal Academy of Arts?

□ **A)** Claudette Johnson

□ **B)** Marlene Smith

□ **C)** Lubaina Himid

□ **D)** Sonia Boyce

24. Which unexpected brand began showing at London Fashion Week in 2005?

    ☐ **A)** Topshop

    ☐ **B)** Adidas

    ☐ **C)** Hunter

    ☐ **D)** Barbour

25. Which provocative artist or artists depicted Jesus Christ in a Union flag loincloth in 2009?

    ☐ **A)** Jeremy Deller

    ☐ **B)** Michael Landy

    ☐ **C)** Gilbert and George

    ☐ **D)** Sarah Lucas

A 209

8. Film

Especially internationally, the reputation of contemporary British cinema can often be reduced to Richard Curtis romcoms, Hugh Grant, Harry Potter and the endless revolutions of James Bond: pale, male and – let's be honest – just a little bit stale.

While we won't deny that that's a key part of our culture, the history of British film, spanning over a century, is more vibrant than the outsize footprint of *Four Weddings and a Funeral* and *Casino Royale* would have you believe.

After all, the world's first moving picture was shot in Leeds in 1888. Britain's first cinema opened on Regent Street in London in February 1896. One hundred years later, British studios had earned a reputation for stellar special effects and production designers.

Many titans of cinema – such as Alfred Hitchcock, Christopher Nolan, Ridley Scott, Cary Grant and Charlie Chaplin – were British-born, although they made it big in the United States. Today British actors appear in starring or supporting roles in very nearly 70 per cent of the 200 highest-earning films from 2011 to 2020.

Diversity remains a key concern for the industry, with women, people of colour and those from working-class backgrounds woefully under-represented in both production and on-screen roles. But change is underway, led by the success of actors like Dev Patel, Daniel Kaluuya and Michaela Coel.

More money is being invested in British film than ever before, with £5.64 billion spent on film and prestige television productions in the UK in 2021 – the highest ever amount reported. We can't complain of having nothing to watch, at least.

A. 212

Questions

1. What is the name of Paul McGann's character in Bruce Robinson's cult film *Withnail and I*?

- ☐ **A)** Martin
- ☐ **B)** Uncle Monty
- ☐ **C)** Marwood
- ☐ **D)** Mondegreen

2. Which of the following films is NOT based on work by the novelist Daphne du Maurier?

- ☐ **A)** *The Birds*
- ☐ **B)** *Don't Look Now*
- ☐ **C)** *My Cousin Rachel*
- ☐ **D)** *The Third Man*

3. What name is given to a character in every Richard Curtis film, as part of a long-running grudge?

- ☐ **A)** Bernard
- ☐ **B)** Hugh
- ☐ **C)** Richard
- ☐ **D)** Charles

4. Which of the following is NOT a real gadget given to James Bond by Q-Branch?

    ☐ **A)** The attack sofa

    ☐ **B)** The aqualung briefcase

    ☐ **C)** The explosive toothpaste

    ☐ **D)** The knife shoe

5. Which film did Radiohead's Jonny Greenwood NOT write the score for?

    ☐ **A)** *Spencer*

    ☐ **B)** *The Power of the Dog*

    ☐ **C)** *Norwegian Wood*

    ☐ **D)** *Churchill*

6. *Trainspotting* was the biggest British movie of 1996, despite a budget of under £2 million. The sequel was titled *T2 Trainspotting* – but what's the title of the novel by Irvine Welsh?

    ☐ **A)** *Porno*

    ☐ **B)** *Crime*

    ☐ **C)** *Filth*

    ☐ **D)** *Glue*

7. Including *No Time to Die*, finally released in 2021 after many delays, how many official James Bond films have there been?

    ☐ **A)** 27

    ☐ **B)** 25

    ☐ **C)** 30

    ☐ **D)** 23

8. Which British actor does NOT appear in the Harry Potter films?

- ☐ **A)** Helen Mirren
- ☐ **B)** Carolyn Pickles
- ☐ **C)** Julie Walters
- ☐ **D)** Maggie Smith

9. Who of the below is NOT a character in Monty Python's *Life of Brian*?

- ☐ **A)** Deadly Dirk
- ☐ **B)** The Black Knight
- ☐ **C)** Mr Big Nose
- ☐ **D)** Bigus Dickus

10. Judi Dench won an Oscar for her supporting role as Queen Elizabeth I in *Shakespeare in Love*. How many minutes was she on screen?

- ☐ **A)** Less than 2 minutes
- ☐ **B)** 8 minutes
- ☐ **C)** 12 minutes
- ☐ **D)** 22 minutes

11. In which Yorkshire city is *The Full Monty* set?

- ☐ **A)** Leeds
- ☐ **B)** Bradford
- ☐ **C)** Doncaster
- ☐ **D)** Sheffield

12. Why did Julie Andrews originally turn down the part of Mary Poppins?

    ☐ **A)** She was pregnant

    ☐ **B)** She was committed to *My Fair Lady* in the West End

    ☐ **C)** She thought the character was sexist

    ☐ **D)** She hated Dick Van Dyke

13. What was the highest-grossing film of 1964?

    ☐ **A)** *The Pink Panther*

    ☐ **B)** *Goldfinger*

    ☐ **C)** *Mary Poppins*

    ☐ **D)** *A Hard Day's Night*

14. What was the debut film of Guy Ritchie?

    ☐ **A)** *Lock, Stock and Two Smoking Barrels*

    ☐ **B)** *Revolver*

    ☐ **C)** *RocknRolla*

    ☐ **D)** *The Gentlemen*

15. Which London street was the inspiration, primary setting and namesake for a quirky 2023 romcom?

    ☐ **A)** Baker Street

    ☐ **B)** Rye Lane

    ☐ **C)** Abbey Road

    ☐ **D)** Brick Lane

16. Shirley Bassey is the only singer to have recorded more than one Bond theme song. There's *Diamonds are Forever*, *Goldfinger* – what is the third?

    ☐ **A)** *Moonraker*

    ☐ **B)** *The Man with the Golden Gun*

    ☐ **C)** *Mr Kiss Kiss Bang Bang*

    ☐ **D)** *Never Say Never Again*

17. Set in the industrial north of England, Ken Loach's classic film *Kes* was about the relationship between a boy and his animal companion. What was it?

    ☐ **A)** Dog

    ☐ **B)** Horse

    ☐ **C)** Bird

    ☐ **D)** Fox

18. Who of the below has NOT been played by Benedict Cumberbatch?

    ☐ **A)** Tudor courtier William Carey

    ☐ **B)** English artist Louis Wain

    ☐ **C)** Former prime minister William Pitt the Elder

    ☐ **D)** Charles Darwin

19. What was the first feature film of Scottish director Bill Forsyth?

    ☐ **A)** *Gregory's Girl*

    ☐ **B)** *That Sinking Feeling*

    ☐ **C)** *Comfort and Joy*

    ☐ **D)** *Local Hero*

20. Which classic British horror film was remade by Hollywood in 2006?

    ☐ **A)** *The Wicker Man*

    ☐ **B)** *Peeping Tom*

    ☐ **C)** *Dead of Night*

    ☐ **D)** *Satan's Slave*

21. Director Alfred Hitchcock was said to have many phobias. Which of the below did he NOT claim?

    ☐ **A)** Fear of crowds

    ☐ **B)** Fear of eggs

    ☐ **C)** Fear of the dark

    ☐ **D)** Fear of dogs

22. Beloved singleton Bridget Jones filled pages of her diary debating between Hugh Grant and Colin Firth's characters – but which foreign-born actor subbed in to complete the love triangle in 2016's *Bridget Jones's Baby*?

    ☐ **A)** Hugh Jackman

    ☐ **B)** Patrick Dempsey

    ☐ **C)** Bradley Cooper

    ☐ **D)** Ryan Gosling

23. By what name is Edgar Wright's genre comedy trilogy, starting with *Shaun of the Dead* in 2004, known?

    ☐ **A)** Edgar Wright vs. the World

    ☐ **B)** Not the Bill

    ☐ **C)** Zombrit

    ☐ **D)** Three Flavours Cornetto

24. *Brooklyn* – based on the 2009 novel by Colm Tóibín, about the lives of Irish migrants in the US – was named Best British Film at the 2016 BATFAs, but in which decade is it set?

- ☐ **A)** The 1930s
- ☐ **B)** The 1940s
- ☐ **C)** The 1950s
- ☐ **D)** The 1960s

25. Which young British actor had his international breakthrough in J. J. Abrams' *Star Wars* reboot?

- ☐ **A)** Moses Ingram
- ☐ **B)** Lucien Laviscount
- ☐ **C)** David Jonsson
- ☐ **D)** John Boyega

A. 212

9. TV

While watching television is of course a universal pastime, it seems like a peculiarly British stroke of madness to spend the night in front of the telly watching other people spend the night in front of the telly. Yet the enormous, decade-long popularity of Channel 4's *Gogglebox* is testament to the central importance of TV in life in the UK.

Britons are behind some of the best television series in the history of the medium, often forging a path for the US and other countries to follow in. The mockumentary format of *The Office* changed comedy, while *House of Cards* and *Veep* both snuck that black British humour into the White House like a Trojan horse. Even the titanic *Succession* has its roots in the quintessentially British odd-couple sitcom *Peep Show*.

And while *EastEnders* and *Emmerdale* may not have gained the global following of Australia's *Neighbours*, Britain's procedural dramas like *Foyle's War*, *Broadchurch*, *Line of Duty*, *The Fall*, *Luther*, *Bodyguard* and *Happy Valley* have all been received well overseas, adding to the impression of British authorities as professionally competent (if personally flawed).

Television is perhaps our most well-received export, or at least the one that we have had to fight the least to impose overseas. It's not for nothing that the BBC World Service was originally titled the BBC Empire Service.

But one of the great charms of British TV is that while we're spoiled for choice when it comes to high-quality comedy and drama, we seem equally content with any old tosh. Some of Britain's most popular programmes, *Gogglebox* among them, appear to have a production budget equal to a leaving collection for a not especially popular colleague.

Often audiences may find themselves quite literally watching paint dry, as the astonishing proliferation of DIY programmes demonstrates – or naked people, revealed by increments in front of a pink-faced Anna Richardson on *Naked Attraction*.

It adds up to an endearing mix of high and low, brilliance and banality, that somehow manages to sum up Britishness better than any history lesson or royal address. What other nation would entertain the idea of a time-travelling phone box* for forty seasons over sixty years?

A. 215

* Yes, we know it's a police box. Just checking you're paying attention.

Questions

1. Who was the third Doctor Who?
- ☐ **A)** William Hartnell
- ☐ **B)** Patrick Troughton
- ☐ **C)** Jon Pertwee
- ☐ **D)** Tom Baker

2. What was the name of the since-abandoned Mr Blobby theme park?
- ☐ **A)** Crinkley Bottom
- ☐ **B)** Splotchy Face
- ☐ **C)** Gurning Grin
- ☐ **D)** Googly Eyes

3. Which TV show has generated the most complaints to Ofcom in its history?
- ☐ **A)** *Coronation Street*
- ☐ **B)** *Love Island*
- ☐ **C)** *Good Morning Britain*
- ☐ **D)** *Britain's Got Talent*

4. Which of the below was NOT a TV channel in 1965?
- ☐ **A)** BBC1
- ☐ **B)** BBC2
- ☐ **C)** Granada/ITV
- ☐ **D)** Channel 4

5. What was the name of Chris Morris's satirical news show?

☐ **A)** *Brass Eye*

☐ **B)** *True Peter*

☐ **C)** *Not the Six o'Clock News*

☐ **D)** *The News at Thirteen*

6. Where was the location used for Kingsroad in *Game of Thrones*, and for many other scenes of the HBO series?

☐ **A)** Northern Ireland

☐ **B)** Wales

☐ **C)** Scotland

☐ **D)** England

7. What was the famous catchphrase of children's television programme *Blue Peter*?

☐ **A)** 'Bad dog!'

☐ **B)** 'That's not for eating.'

☐ **C)** 'Ask your parents first.'

☐ **D)** 'Here's one I made earlier.'

8. Which of the below was considered as a name for Rowan Atkinson's hapless character Mr Bean?

☐ **A)** Monsieur Haricot

☐ **B)** Mr Green

☐ **C)** Mr Cauliflower

☐ **D)** Mr Legume

9. In 1990, an episode of which show was removed from broadcasting and home video distribution for reasons of taste?

☐ **A)** *The Queen's Nose*

☐ **B)** *Pingu*

☐ **C)** *Grange Hill*

☐ **D)** *The Simpsons*

10. What was the title of the 2020 ITV dramatization of the 2021 *Who Wants to be a Millionaire* cheating scandal?

☐ **A)** *Quiz*

☐ **B)** *The Million-dollar Question*

☐ **C)** *Your Final Answer*

☐ **D)** *The Millionaire Major*

11. Who of the following *Succession* cast members is NOT British?

☐ **A)** Matthew Macfadyen

☐ **B)** Annabelle Dexter-Jones

☐ **C)** Brian Cox

☐ **D)** Sarah Snook

12. What, in *Peep Show*, is given as one of two reasons against listening to the public?

☐ **A)** Cauliflower at Christmas

☐ **B)** The popularity of Coldplay

☐ **C)** Cliff Richard's 'The Millennium Prayer' reaching number one

☐ **D)** Former Radio 1 DJ Chris Evans's career

13. Who was the first winner of *Big Brother* in 2000?

- ☐ **A)** Craig Phillips
- ☐ **B)** Anna Nolan
- ☐ **C)** Brian Dowling
- ☐ **D)** Kate Lawler

14. Which bright young British actor did NOT get their start on *Skins*?

- ☐ **A)** Nicholas Hoult
- ☐ **B)** Dev Patel
- ☐ **C)** Will Poulter
- ☐ **D)** Daniel Kaluuya

15. 'Listen very carefully, for I shall say this only once' is a slogan from which British sitcom?

- ☐ **A)** *Fawlty Towers*
- ☐ **B)** *'Allo 'Allo*
- ☐ **C)** *Blackadder*
- ☐ **D)** *Dad's Army*

16. Who replaced Sandi Toksvig as co-host of *The Great British Bake Off* in 2020?

- ☐ **A)** Mel Giedroyc
- ☐ **B)** Sue Perkins
- ☐ **C)** Noel Fielding
- ☐ **D)** Matt Lucas

17. Which singer regularly played herself in *Absolutely Fabulous*?

    ☐ **A)** Adele

    ☐ **B)** Madonna

    ☐ **C)** Cilla Black

    ☐ **D)** Lulu

18. In which year was the final weekly episode of *Top of the Pops* shown on TV?

    ☐ **A)** 1996

    ☐ **B)** 1998

    ☐ **C)** 2002

    ☐ **D)** 2006

19. What is the first name of Mrs Brown of *Mrs Brown's Boys*?

    ☐ **A)** Deirdre

    ☐ **B)** Agnes

    ☐ **C)** Nora

    ☐ **D)** Kathleen

20. In *Fleabag*, what do Phoebe Waller-Bridge's character and her sister agree that they would trade for five years of their life?

    ☐ **A)** The perfect man

    ☐ **B)** The perfect body

    ☐ **C)** Limitless money

    ☐ **D)** Endless wishes

21. Which actress has NOT played Queen Elizabeth II in *The Crown*?

- ☐ **A)** Claire Foy
- ☐ **B)** Imelda Staunton
- ☐ **C)** Olivia Colman
- ☐ **D)** Helen Mirren

22. Channel 4's *Come Dine with Me* has been commissioned in 46 territories across the world, with over 17,000 episodes produced globally. Which of the below is NOT a real title of the show?

- ☐ **A)** *Without a Napkin*
- ☐ **B)** *A Game of Pans*
- ☐ **C)** *What Can I Bring?*
- ☐ **D)** *Coming to Eat*

23. What 1992 Hallowe'en night broadcast sparked a furore for the BBC?

- ☐ **A)** Michael Parkinson pretended to be possessed by a demon live on air
- ☐ **B)** *The Omen* was broadcast pre-watershed due to a programming error
- ☐ **C)** *Don't Look Now* aired with the controversial sex scene
- ☐ **D)** It coincided with a party leaders' debate

24. What is the name of the main pub where the Shelbys meet in *Peaky Blinders*?

- ☐ **A)** The Anchor
- ☐ **B)** The Aigburth Arms
- ☐ **C)** The Garrison Tavern
- ☐ **D)** The Rising Sun

25. If you live on Albert Square, like the characters in *EastEnders*, what's your postcode?

☐ **A)** E20
☐ **B)** E1
☐ **C)** E2
☐ **D)** E1W

A. 215

10. Politics

When it comes to politics, there are two kinds of people. You either follow all the goings-on down at Westminster like it's a sitcom that you can't wait to catch up with, where you love to hate the characters and you know all their backstories – or else you're trying to tune it out as much as you possibly can.

After all, how much impact can politics have on your day-to-day life, really?

Maybe that explains the position we're in now. It used to be as though we had a shared, society-wide understanding that we had politics for a reason: yes, it might be boring and frustrating and often quite silly – but we made do for the sake of democracy, and governance, and each other.

Now, whether you're sprinting to keep up with current events or burying your head deeper into the sand, both positions seem to be getting increasingly hard to maintain. In recent years, the political landscape has become so polarized, frenetic and fraught you wonder what even the politicians themselves are getting out of it.

In 2015, then prime minister David Cameron said Britain had a 'simple and inescapable choice: stability and strong government' with the Conservatives 'or chaos with Ed Miliband'. We didn't end up with Ed Miliband, but we have certainly not wanted for chaos, despite the Tories being in charge.

In less than a decade, we've been through a wrenching referendum, a deadly pandemic, back-to-back lockdowns, sweeping strikes, unprecedented heat and biting inflation. In less than a *year*, we've had three prime ministers. One, you may recall, was outlasted by a lettuce – yet still managed to wreak havoc on the economy.

Regardless of where you sit on the political spectrum, the people tasked with steering us through haven't always seemed to have had our best interests at heart. 'Stability and strong government' has not felt like an option that's been on the table. Indeed, some of the leadership we've had has made that in Armando Iannucci's satires look strong and stable.

Surveyed in May 2023 about prime minister Rishi Sunak's pledge to achieve 'integrity, professionalism and accountability at every level' of government, nearly 60 per cent of Britons polled said he had been either mostly or completely unsuccessful.

Given the displays from some of our representatives, it's not surprising that some of us have checked out of politics altogether. They need to get better writers in, and characters and stories we can relate to, because these last few seasons have jumped the shark.

It speaks to the growing disconnect between politics and people, and not just in Britain. Many people have lost faith in these institutions and systems as a means of achieving positive change, or even as having any bearing on their lives.

There's only so long that you can ride a roller coaster without becoming hooked on the drama, trying to anticipate the next twist – or squeezing your eyes shut, hoping against hope that it will all be over soon.

But politics doesn't have to feel like something happening to us, something we're either spectators or prisoners of. Learning to pay attention, on our terms, can help us to feel more aware – and, with it, more empowered. So, let's start: who's the prime minister again?

A · 217

Questions

1. Who is generally considered the first prime minister of the United Kingdom?

    ☐ **A)** Robert Walpole

    ☐ **B)** Spencer Compton

    ☐ **C)** Henry Pelham

    ☐ **D)** Thomas Pelham-Holles

2. What song was adopted as the unofficial anthem for the Labour leader Jeremy Corbyn?

    ☐ **A)** 'We are the Champions' by Queen

    ☐ **B)** 'Us and Them' by Pink Floyd

    ☐ **C)** 'Seven Nation Army' by The White Stripes

    ☐ **D)** 'Shiny Happy People' by REM

3. Who of the below spent approximately 40 per cent of their life as PM?

    ☐ **A)** William Pitt the Younger

    ☐ **B)** William Pitt the Elder

    ☐ **C)** Robert Walpole

    ☐ **D)** Margaret Thatcher

4. Which prime minister introduced the NHS?

☐ **A)** Clement Attlee

☐ **B)** Winston Churchill

☐ **C)** Neville Chamberlain

☐ **D)** Anthony Eden

5. In what year did the Democratic Unionist Party form in Northern Ireland?

☐ **A)** 1969

☐ **B)** 1970

☐ **C)** 1972

☐ **D)** 1971

6. In October 1988, the British government banned the broadcast of the voices of representatives of Sinn Féin and several Irish republican and loyalist groups. How many years was the ban in place?

☐ **A)** 3

☐ **B)** 6

☐ **C)** 9

☐ **D)** 12

7. Which party won the UK general election of 1945, just before the end of the Second World War?

☐ **A)** Labour

☐ **B)** Whig

☐ **C)** Conservative

☐ **D)** Liberal

8. Who was the United Kingdom's first ever Black peer?

☐ **A)** Valerie Amos

☐ **B)** David Pitt

☐ **C)** Learie Constantine

☐ **D)** Patricia Scotland

9. All these prime ministers died while in office, but who is the only British prime minister to have been assassinated?

☐ **A)** George Canning

☐ **B)** Spencer Perceval

☐ **C)** Henry John Temple

☐ **D)** Henry Pelham

10. Before entering politics, what invention did Margaret Thatcher help pioneer?

☐ **A)** Mr Whippy ice cream

☐ **B)** The mackintosh jacket

☐ **C)** The electric lightbulb

☐ **D)** The Thermos flask

11. In 1988, Margaret Thatcher's Conservative party passed the notorious Section 28 laws banning the 'promotion of homosexuality' in schools and public libraries. When was that legislation finally repealed?

☐ **A)** 1995

☐ **B)** 1998

☐ **C)** 2003

☐ **D)** 2005

12. What was the vision set out in the Labour Party's 1997 general election in its campaign song?

 ☐ **A)** 'Mr Blue Sky' by ELO

 ☐ **B)** 'Ghost Town' by The Specials

 ☐ **C)** 'Beautiful Day' by U2

 ☐ **D)** 'Things Can Only Get Better' by D:Ream

13. Which party won control of the Senedd in the 2021 election?

 ☐ **A)** Labour

 ☐ **B)** Conservative

 ☐ **C)** Plaid Cymru

 ☐ **D)** Liberal Democrats

14. Which of the below is NOT a component of the PPE degree, often studied by aspiring politicians?

 ☐ **A)** Politics

 ☐ **B)** Philosophy

 ☐ **C)** English Literature

 ☐ **D)** Economics

15. When Jacob Rees-Mogg resigned from government, in a handwritten letter, what historic October date did he give?

 ☐ **A)** St Crispin's Day

 ☐ **B)** Old Michaelmas Day

 ☐ **C)** Feast Day of St Keyne

 ☐ **D)** Punkie Night

16. How long was Liz Truss prime minister?

- ☐ **A)** 43 days
- ☐ **B)** 47 days
- ☐ **C)** 50 days
- ☐ **D)** 52 days

17. As an 18-year-old schoolgirl, which politician beat Julio Iglesias to win the 1970 Eurovision Song Contest for Ireland?

- ☐ **A)** Siobhan Fahey
- ☐ **B)** Dana Scallon
- ☐ **C)** Maureen Nolan
- ☐ **D)** Enya Brennan

18. Which politician's Twitter gaffe continues to be commemorated annually on the platform?

- ☐ **A)** Ed Miliband
- ☐ **B)** Sadiq Khan
- ☐ **C)** Ed Balls
- ☐ **D)** Yvette Cooper

19. What, to widespread bemusement, did prime minister Theresa May give as the 'naughtiest thing' she'd ever done as a child in a television interview in 2017?

- ☐ **A)** She ran through fields of wheat
- ☐ **B)** She studied too hard at school
- ☐ **C)** She shoplifted some sweets
- ☐ **D)** She littered, once

20. Who was dubbed 'Mother of the House' in recognition of her status as the longest continuously serving woman MP?

   ☐ **A)** Yvette Cooper

   ☐ **B)** Margaret Beckett

   ☐ **C)** Rosie Winterton

   ☐ **D)** Harriet Harman

21. In 2017, the Darth Vader-looking, satirical-ish? political candidate Lord Buckethead made his return to politics to go up against Theresa May. In the 1987 election, Buckethead received 131 votes; in 1992, he won 107. How many did he win at his comeback in 2017?

   ☐ **A)** 134

   ☐ **B)** 249

   ☐ **C)** 700

   ☐ **D)** 1,225

22. At the height of Britain's 2020 coronavirus pandemic, what reason did the prime minister's former chief advisor Dominic Cummings give for breaking lockdown rules and driving his entire family 30 miles to Barnard Castle?

   ☐ **A)** He was testing his eyesight

   ☐ **B)** His wife was ill

   ☐ **C)** He was being a good father

   ☐ **D)** He did not believe the rules applied to him

23. Britain went to the polls twice in a single year in 1974. In February, the Conservative prime minister Edward Heath called an election, hoping to strengthen his majority and quell civil unrest. It didn't quite go to plan – but which, of these strident soundbites, was cemented as his catchphrase?

- ☐ **A)** 'This time of strife has got to stop.'
- ☐ **B)** 'There's a lot to be done. For heaven's sake, let's get on with it.'
- ☐ **C)** 'Who governs Britain?'
- ☐ **D)** 'It's time for you to say to the extremists, the militants, and the plain and simply misguided: we've had enough.'

24. What was the pre-dawn 'Portillo moment' of the 1997 general election, considered one of the most dramatic political TV moments ever?

- ☐ **A)** The polling was precisely accurate
- ☐ **B)** Portillo abruptly conceded his safe seat to Stephen Twigg
- ☐ **C)** Portillo walked out of the live broadcast
- ☐ **D)** Labour candidate Stephen Twigg defeated Conservative cabinet minister Michael Portillo

25. Which party gained control of the Northern Ireland Assembly in May 2022?

- ☐ **A)** Sinn Féin
- ☐ **B)** DUP
- ☐ **C)** Ulster Unionist Party
- ☐ **D)** Alliance Party

A. 217

11. Books

Even if we were to look only at the works of William Shakespeare, Britain would have a rich literary heritage. As it is, of course, it goes well beyond the Bard.

What is most striking about Britain's literary tradition is how directly it extends from the past to today. Though the countryside around Stratford-upon-Avon has been transformed, it is still possible to glimpse the inspiration for *A Midsummer Night's Dream* in the surrounding forests.

More immediate is his impact on language. Shakespeare's writing greatly contributed to the standardization of spelling and grammar, while many words and phrases he invented are still in use today. 'Zany', to give just one example, is from *Love's Labour's Lost* (a derivative of the Italian name Giovanni).

Charles Dickens was moved to capture the teeming life of London in the nineteenth century. Today the city's promise, opportunity and inequality are similarly high stakes, inspiring writers like Monica Ali and John Lanchester. The sharp social commentary that powered Jane Austen's and E. M. Forster's novels can now be read in Zadie Smith and Bernardine Evaristo. Kazuo Ishiguro has named among his influences Charlotte Brontë, British folk songs and Arthurian legend.

It amounts to a centuries-old tradition of reading and writing that is continually pulling from the past to comment on the present, and which imagines the future. According to a 2020 YouGov survey, two in five (43 per cent) Britons say that they read for pleasure at least once a week; a third (35 per cent) read more frequently.

Books are, proudly, a pillar of our national identity – just look at our towering bedside to-be-read piles. But how much of what you read do you remember?

A. 221

Questions

1. Which fantastical head-scratcher from Roald Dahl did students from Leicester University attempt to solve in 2013?

- ☐ **A)** How many sleeping pills are needed to drug a forest's worth of pheasants?
- ☐ **B)** How many seagulls are needed to lift James's giant peach?
- ☐ **C)** Is there any link between precociousness and telekinesis?
- ☐ **D)** How much suction did the pipe that sucked up Augustus Gloop need?

2. *Midnight's Children* and *Satanic Verses* author Salman Rushdie used to work as a copywriter. Which famous slogan did he come up with?

- ☐ **A)** 'Have a break. Have a Kit Kat'
- ☐ **B)** 'Aero: Irresistibubble'
- ☐ **C)** 'It's not Terry's. It's mine'
- ☐ **D)** 'The lighter way to enjoy chocolate'

3. Simon Armitage was made Poet Laureate in 2019, taking over from Carol Ann Duffy. But who had she replaced in the role?

- ☐ **A)** Andrew Motion
- ☐ **B)** Ted Hughes
- ☐ **C)** Seamus Heaney
- ☐ **D)** Philip Larkin

4. What was Jilly Cooper talking about when she said this: 'Some of them are a load of crap. Mostly, though, they're wonderful.'

☐ **A)** Mills & Boon romance novels

☐ **B)** Horses

☐ **C)** Men

☐ **D)** Teachers

5. Which Dickens novel is the only one to have a female narrator?

☐ **A)** *Bleak House*

☐ **B)** *The Pickwick Papers*

☐ **C)** *Little Dorrit*

☐ **D)** *Our Mutual Friend*

6. How did Agatha Christie make headlines in 1926?

☐ **A)** She published *The Murder of Roger Ackroyd*, her most famous book

☐ **B)** A murder was committed that mirrored one of her plots exactly

☐ **C)** She announced her retirement from writing to become an archaeologist

☐ **D)** She went missing for 11 days

7. What is the name of Stormzy's publishing imprint?

☐ **A)** #Merky Books

☐ **B)** #F Boris Books

☐ **C)** Boris Bop Books

☐ **D)** Vossi Books

8. One of Enid Blyton's Famous Five is, in fact, a dog. Which one is it?

- ☐ **A)** Dick
- ☐ **B)** Julian
- ☐ **C)** Timmy
- ☐ **D)** George

9. *Alice in Wonderland* author Lewis Carroll suffered from a rare disorder that was an inspiration for his book. What was it?

- ☐ **A)** Klüver-Bucy syndrome, which makes people try to eat non-food items
- ☐ **B)** Todd's syndrome, which affects perception of size
- ☐ **C)** Empty Sella syndrome, which causes chronic headaches
- ☐ **D)** Hallucinogen persisting perception disorder, which causes visual disturbances and flashbacks

10. Why did Charlotte Brontë's dedication of *Jane Eyre* to William Thackeray, one of her favourite authors, cause embarrassment?

- ☐ **A)** Thackeray refused to read books by women
- ☐ **B)** Thackeray's name was spelt incorrectly
- ☐ **C)** He saw in *Jane Eyre* a plagiarism of his own *Vanity Fair*
- ☐ **D)** His own wife was secretly mentally ill, like Bertha Rochester

11. In Douglas Adams's *Hitchhiker's Guide to the Galaxy*, what is the name of the depressed and paranoid android?

- ☐ **A)** Martin
- ☐ **B)** Arthur
- ☐ **C)** Stephen
- ☐ **D)** Max

12. In the Harry Potter series, who is the author of the textbook *A History of Magic*?

    ☐ **A)** Penny Pendragon

    ☐ **B)** Arthur Weasley

    ☐ **C)** Bathilda Bagshot

    ☐ **D)** Minerva McGonagall

13. What was *Chronicles of Narnia* author C. S. Lewis's middle name?

    ☐ **A)** Simpson

    ☐ **B)** Samuel

    ☐ **C)** Staples

    ☐ **D)** Smith

14. Which classic English novel opens with the famous first line 'Last night I dreamt I went to Manderley again . . .'

    ☐ **A)** *Rebecca*

    ☐ **B)** *Emma*

    ☐ **C)** *Jane Eyre*

    ☐ **D)** *Mrs Dalloway*

15. The screenplay for *Chitty Chitty Bang Bang* was co-written by Roald Dahl, but who wrote the children's novel it was loosely based on?

    ☐ **A)** Anthony Burgess

    ☐ **B)** Ian Fleming

    ☐ **C)** Enid Blyton

    ☐ **D)** Arthur Ransome

16. Inspired by A. A. Milne's charming characters of childhood, where are the Pooh-sticks World Championships held?

- ☐ **A)** Norfolk
- ☐ **B)** Oxfordshire
- ☐ **C)** Kent
- ☐ **D)** Devon

17. Which now well-known term did *Middlemarch* author George Eliot coin in an 1862 letter?

- ☐ **A)** Emo
- ☐ **B)** The ick
- ☐ **C)** Sadboy
- ☐ **D)** Pop

18. Political philosopher William Godwin and pioneering feminist author Mary Wollstonecraft welcomed a daughter in 1797 who, too, grew up to be a successful writer. Who was she later known as?

- ☐ **A)** Mary Shelley
- ☐ **B)** Jane Austen
- ☐ **C)** Ann Radcliffe
- ☐ **D)** Charlotte Smith

19. Bernardine Evaristo became the first Black woman to win the Booker Prize in 2019 with which novel?

- ☐ **A)** *Soul Tourists*
- ☐ **B)** *Mr Loverman*
- ☐ **C)** *Lara*
- ☐ **D)** *Girl, Woman, Other*

20. Zadie Smith's *On Beauty* was an update of another classic English novel. What was its first line?

    ☐ **A)** 'It is a truth universally acknowledged, that a single man in possession of a good fortune, must be in want of a new iPhone.'

    ☐ **B)** 'One may as well begin with Jerome's emails to his father.'

    ☐ **C)** 'It was the best of internet connections, it was the worst of internet connections.'

    ☐ **D)** 'I write this sitting in the internet café.'

21. What classic of English literature was originally titled 'First Impressions'?

    ☐ **A)** *Pride and Prejudice*

    ☐ **B)** *Howards End*

    ☐ **C)** *Great Expectations*

    ☐ **D)** *Barchester Towers*

22. Four authors have won the Booker Prize more than once. Who, of the below, has not?

    ☐ **A)** Hilary Mantel

    ☐ **B)** J. M. Coetzee

    ☐ **C)** Peter Carey

    ☐ **D)** Salman Rushdie

23. 'It seems increasingly likely that I really will undertake the expedition that has been preoccupying my imagination now for some days' is the opening sentence of which novel?

☐ **A)** *The Remains of the Day* by Kazuo Ishiguro

☐ **B)** *The End of the Affair* by Graham Greene

☐ **C)** *Atonement* by Ian McEwan

☐ **D)** *The Go-between* by L. P. Hartley

24. Which novel did pop star, podcast host (and Booker Prize keynote speaker) Dua Lipa select as the inaugural pick for her book club?

☐ **A)** *Milkman* by Anna Burns

☐ **B)** *Beautiful World Where Are You* by Sally Rooney

☐ **C)** *Shuggie Bain* by Douglas Stuart

☐ **D)** *Burnt Sugar* by Avni Doshi

25. Which naval captain did Patrick O'Brian base the exploits of the fictional Jack Aubrey on in his book *Master and Commander*?

☐ **A)** Lord Cochrane

☐ **B)** Horatio Hornblower

☐ **C)** Horatio Nelson

☐ **D)** Sir Edward Pellew

A. 221

12. Landscapes and Landmarks

Great Britain is a small island with a lot to see.

Between rolling hills, spectacular mountains, moody moors and staggering cliffs, it contains remarkable geologic diversity within a relatively small area, reflecting centuries of shifting sands. In primeval times, for instance, large parts of central and southern England were under water.

Over time, rocks emerged from beneath the waves to form the country's natural peaks, for example Scafell Pike and the Pennines. The oldest cliffs are on the south-western peninsula, among them Land's End: the multicoloured, tiered sandstones are a visual representation of their extreme age.

With its steep drops, sharp turns and shifting estuaries, the English coastline itself tells a story – one that's 2,000 miles long and more than 185 million years old. The rocks in Scotland are even older, with the Lewisian rocks on the north-west seaboard thought to be close to 3,000 million years old.

For all the natural beauty of the British Isles, however, there is more that is manmade. Between Roman baths, castles, cathedrals and bridges, for as long as there has been human settlement in Britain, there has been striving for beauty.

Another aspect of what makes the British landscape so unique and engrossing is how much we don't know about it. Even our manmade landmarks may be in large part a mystery to us.

Stonehenge, for example, is a mighty circle of stones that was erected in the late Neolithic period, around 2500 BC. The largest of the standing sarsen stones are huge, around 13 feet high, almost 7 feet wide, and weighing around 25 tons. The question of why and how they were transported by our ancestors continues to be speculated over today, inside every car that passes by on the A303.

At a time when all of human history and knowledge seems instantly available, there's a real pleasure to being able to lose ourselves in the past. But how much do you know for sure?

A. 223

Questions

1. There are forty-six 'Areas of Outstanding Natural Beauty' across England, Wales and Northern Ireland. Of those forty-six, how many are NOT in England?

    ☐ **A)** 13
    ☐ **B)** 5
    ☐ **C)** 23
    ☐ **D)** 31

2. Approximately how far away from the sea can you get in England?

    ☐ **A)** 50 miles
    ☐ **B)** 60 miles
    ☐ **C)** 75 miles
    ☐ **D)** 90 miles

3. Where in London is Windrush Square, named for the people who settled there after arriving on HMT *Empire Windrush* on 22 June 1948?

    ☐ **A)** Dalston
    ☐ **B)** Peckham
    ☐ **C)** Ealing
    ☐ **D)** Brixton

4. What was the first skyscraper in the British Isles when it opened in 1906?

    ☐ **A)** The Guinness Storehouse

    ☐ **B)** Royal Liver Building

    ☐ **C)** The NatWest Tower

    ☐ **D)** Senate House

5. In 2002, the 4,600-year-old grave was discovered of what became known as 'the Amesbury Archer'. A younger man's skeleton was found nearby. What, in 2022, was found to most likely be their relationship?

    ☐ **A)** Brothers

    ☐ **B)** Father and son

    ☐ **C)** Great-grandfather and great-grandson

    ☐ **D)** No DNA link is identifiable

6. In which cave was the biggest concentration of 'anti-witch' etchings ever found in the UK uncovered in 2019?

    ☐ **A)** Creswell Crags

    ☐ **B)** Wookey Hole

    ☐ **C)** Mother Ludlam's Hole

    ☐ **D)** Mother Shipton's Cave

7. Which is the 'real' Downton Abbey?

    ☐ **A)** Blickling Hall, Norfolk

    ☐ **B)** Highclere Castle, Hampshire

    ☐ **C)** Mamhead House, Devon

    ☐ **D)** Chatsworth House, Derbyshire

8. What is the roughly equivalent area of the Stonehenge World Heritage Site in Wiltshire?

□ **A)** Twenty standard football pitches

□ **B)** The entire Glastonbury festival site

□ **C)** All four terminals of Heathrow

□ **D)** Seven and a half times the size of New York's Central Park

9. Which Scottish mountain was the site of an eighteenth-century experiment to measure the mass of the Earth using a pendulum?

□ **A)** Schiehallion

□ **B)** Buachaille Etive Mòr

□ **C)** Cairn Gorm

□ **D)** Ben Nevis

10. Which of the below rivers is longest?

□ **A)** River Thames

□ **B)** River Severn

□ **C)** River Trent

□ **D)** River Wye

11. Which of the below is NOT the actual name of an English village?

□ **A)** Westward Ho!

□ **B)** Brokenwind

□ **C)** Hutton-le-Hole

□ **D)** Barton in the Beans

12. Which London establishment had the UK's first escalators, installed in 1898?

    ☐ **A)** National Gallery

    ☐ **B)** The Royal Holloway College

    ☐ **C)** Harrods

    ☐ **D)** Victoria and Albert Museum

13. In 2017, the historic clipper *Cutty Sark* was given a new figure-head, inspired by a Robert Burns poem. What is her name?

    ☐ **A)** Nannie the witch

    ☐ **B)** Ariel the mermaid

    ☐ **C)** Tam o'Shanter

    ☐ **D)** Maggie the Auld Mare

14. By what name is the Elizabeth Tower better known?

    ☐ **A)** The Shard

    ☐ **B)** The Tower of London

    ☐ **C)** 20 Fenchurch Street

    ☐ **D)** Big Ben

15. What is Cooper Hill, Gloucestershire County, best known for?

    ☐ **A)** Earliest ancient Briton burial ground

    ☐ **B)** Chalk drawing

    ☐ **C)** Largest ever discovery of Roman treasure

    ☐ **D)** Annual cheese-rolling competition

16. The British Museum first opened its doors in 1759, and attracted around 75 visitors a day. How many people visited on its busiest ever day in 2013?

    ☐ **A)** Nearly 35,000

    ☐ **B)** 5,000

    ☐ **C)** 10,000

    ☐ **D)** Over 50,000

17. Not long after it was erected in Gateshead in 1998, the 65-foot-high Angel of the North was defaced by some creative locals. What with?

    ☐ **A)** A Union Jack

    ☐ **B)** A Newcastle United shirt

    ☐ **C)** Toilet roll

    ☐ **D)** Wings

18. Which is the largest loch in Scotland by surface area, by some distance?

    ☐ **A)** Loch Maree

    ☐ **B)** Loch Awe

    ☐ **C)** Loch Lomond

    ☐ **D)** Loch Lochy

19. What is the name of the principal river that flows through Cardiff?

    ☐ **A)** Ely

    ☐ **B)** Rhymney

    ☐ **C)** Towy

    ☐ **D)** Taff

20. What was the nickname of the late architect Zaha Hadid?

☐ **A)** Queen of the Curve

☐ **B)** The Duchess of Design

☐ **C)** The Empress of the Outline

☐ **D)** The Lady of the Line

21. Which of these is NOT a nickname for a London tower?

☐ **A)** The Gherkin

☐ **B)** The Cheese Grater

☐ **C)** The Walkie-talkie

☐ **D)** The Microwave

22. Which British city shares its name with a site on the moon?

☐ **A)** York

☐ **B)** Leeds

☐ **C)** Chester

☐ **D)** Birmingham

23. What figure does NOT appear drawn in chalk on an English hillside?

☐ **A)** A horse

☐ **B)** A swan

☐ **C)** A kiwi

☐ **D)** A club-wielding giant

24. Which of the following landmarks does NOT appear on album artwork?

□ **A)** Battersea Power Station

□ **B)** Tower Bridge

□ **C)** Camden Market

□ **D)** London Bridge

25. By what name is MV *Monte Rosa* better known?

□ **A)** *Empire Windrush*

□ **B)** *Cutty Sark*

□ **C)** *Mary Rose*

□ **D)** *Endeavour*

A. 223

13. The Monarchy

The royals may be the best-known Britons in the world – sorry, Rita Ora – but they also defy easy explanation. Yes, they're sort of celebrities, in that we are fascinated by insights into their daily lives, follow their family drama like it's a soap opera, and queue for hours just to glimpse them from afar.

But the increasingly glitzy, gossipy profile of the Windsors, as their secrets and tensions spill over via Hollywood, distracts from their enormous power and the way they came to amass it. They may be on text-message terms with Beyoncé and taking tea with Paddington Bear and other luminaries, but the royal family are not like regular members of the rich and famous.

Their influence today dates back centuries to the reign of William the Conquerer, and since that time they have been proactive about not only amassing power and wealth but protecting it. Historically this was achieved through the British empire, built with slave labour and the looting of foreign countries.

According to some recent reports, the royal family are the public faces of an empire still valued at £23 billion.

For the modern-day royal family, brand management remains a key concern. King George V replaced their historic family name of Saxe-Coburg-Gotha with Windsor during the First World War to distance the British throne from its recent German heritage. Plus, 'Windsor' is easier to fit on a commemorative biscuit tin.

Especially under Queen Elizabeth II, who reigned for seventy years, the royal family has been praised as a source of stability through increasingly turbulent times. But their strictly non-political, corgis-and-crumpets image undermines the secrecy with which they guard details of their wealth and how they exert their influence.

That doesn't mean you can't enjoy the pageantry, the history, the drama, the symbolism. The royal family is British spectacle at its best – enjoy the show. Just don't forget you're footing the bill.

A. 225

Questions

1. What was the secret code name given to the plan for the death of Queen Elizabeth II?

☐ **A)** Operation Morrissey

☐ **B)** Crown Jewels

☐ **C)** Big Ben

☐ **D)** Operation London Bridge

2. What name did Queen Victoria go by before her coronation?

☐ **A)** Drina

☐ **B)** Tori

☐ **C)** Vic

☐ **D)** Albertina

3. What iconic beauty product did Prince Harry memorably name-check in his no-holds-barred, bestselling memoir *Spare*?

☐ **A)** La Mer

☐ **B)** Elizabeth Arden Eight-hour Cream

☐ **C)** Chanel No. 5

☐ **D)** Lanolips

4. The royal family shies away from sharing specifics about its wealth, much of which is tied up in property and trusts. But how much public money does King Charles receive annually in the form of the sovereign grant?

- ☐ **A)** None
- ☐ **B)** £1 million a year
- ☐ **C)** £25 million a year
- ☐ **D)** £86 million a year

5. Which of the below has NOT been reported to be a rule in the royal family?

- ☐ **A)** No playing Monopoly
- ☐ **B)** No eating shellfish out
- ☐ **C)** No tea to be taken after 7 p.m.
- ☐ **D)** No tiaras indoors after 6 p.m., except on your wedding day

6. 'Zadok the Priest' by Handel was sung at King Charles III's coronation and many more before it. George Frideric Handel composed the piece almost 300 years ago, for whose coronation?

- ☐ **A)** King George I
- ☐ **B)** King George II
- ☐ **C)** King George III
- ☐ **D)** King George IV

7. Which species does the monarch lay claim to?

    ☐ **A)** Mute swans

    ☐ **B)** Porpoises

    ☐ **C)** Sturgeons

    ☐ **D)** All of the above

8. What was Henry VII's great-granddaughter Lady Jane Grey otherwise known as?

    ☐ **A)** The seven-year-old queen

    ☐ **B)** The four-foot queen

    ☐ **C)** The nine-day queen

    ☐ **D)** The five o'clock queen

9. King Charles III has what kind of animal named after him?

    ☐ **A)** Frog

    ☐ **B)** Sheep

    ☐ **C)** Gecko

    ☐ **D)** Owl

10. Queen Victoria was raised under the very strict 'Kensington System' of rules developed by her mother and her mother's attendant. What was 18-year-old Victoria's first request as queen?

    ☐ **A)** Less restrictive undergarments

    ☐ **B)** Three meals of mutton

    ☐ **C)** An hour alone

    ☐ **D)** All kinds of sponge cakes, wafers, biscuits, petit fours and a large variety of mixed sweets

11. What astonishing claim did Prince Andrew make during the *Newsnight* interview to clear his name after being accused of having sex with an underage Virginia Giuffre?

- ☐ **A)** He had been unable to sweat for a time after the Falklands War
- ☐ **B)** He had been at Woking Pizza Express in 2001, not Tramp nightclub
- ☐ **C)** He had sometimes stayed with convicted sex offender Jeffrey Epstein because it was convenient
- ☐ **D)** All of the above

12. What is NOT a feature of the royal family's Queen Mary's doll's house?

- ☐ **A)** Running water, and electricity
- ☐ **B)** Musical scores including works by Gustav Holst and John Ireland
- ☐ **C)** A well-stocked wine cellar
- ☐ **D)** A miniature self-portrait by Charlie Chaplin

13. Games are always popular at Christmas. What is the Windsors' quirky tradition at Sandringham?

- ☐ **A)** Weighing themselves on arrival and departure
- ☐ **B)** Getting takeaway on the day after Boxing Day
- ☐ **C)** Wearing civilian clothes such as jeans
- ☐ **D)** A Christmas-day shower, as opposed to a daily bath

14. The royals also famously love to exchange joke presents. Which of the below is NOT a gift Queen Elizabeth II reportedly received for Christmas?

- ☐ **A)** A shower cap saying 'Ain't life a bitch' from Harry
- ☐ **B)** A novelty Christmas sweater from William
- ☐ **C)** A jar of home-made chutney from Kate
- ☐ **D)** A singing toy hamster from Megan

15. What was the disquieting nickname of Edward VII, Queen Elizabeth II's great-grandfather?

- ☐ **A)** Edward the Caresser
- ☐ **B)** Edward the Conquester
- ☐ **C)** Edward the Harasser
- ☐ **D)** Edward the Confessor

16. Which royal wedding had the biggest TV audience globally?

- ☐ **A)** Prince Harry and Meghan Markle
- ☐ **B)** Prince William and Catherine Middleton
- ☐ **C)** Prince Charles and Lady Diana Spencer
- ☐ **D)** Princess Margaret and Antony Armstrong-Jones

17. Which royal, in 2017, held the under-sung title of 'Prime Warden of the Worshipful Company of Fishmongers' (among others, of course)?

- ☐ **A)** Princess Eugenie
- ☐ **B)** Princess Anne
- ☐ **C)** Prince William
- ☐ **D)** Princess Beatrice

18. What was the name of Meghan Markle's lifestyle blog?

☐ **A)** The Tig

☐ **B)** The Tags

☐ **C)** The Tabs

☐ **D)** Toggle

19. How do the Commons and the Crown honour their 'previously contentious relationship' during the state opening of Parliament?

☐ **A)** A ceremonial spilling of (symbolic) blood

☐ **B)** A ceremonial banquet

☐ **C)** A ceremonial recital of the National Anthem

☐ **D)** A ceremonial 'hostage-taking' of an MP

20. Who is highest of the below in the line of succession?

☐ **A)** Prince Harry

☐ **B)** Prince George of Cambridge

☐ **C)** Princess Charlotte of Cambridge

☐ **D)** Prince Louis of Cambridge

21. How old was Mary, Queen of Scots, when she became queen in 1542?

☐ **A)** 6 days old

☐ **B)** 6 weeks old

☐ **C)** 6 years old

☐ **D)** 16 years old

22. King George VI famously enlisted a speech therapist for his stutter. But which George had a dragon tattoo?

- ☐ **A)** King George I
- ☐ **B)** King George III
- ☐ **C)** King George IV
- ☐ **D)** King George V

23. Reigning King Charles has put his own spin on the Greek dish moussaka. What does he use in place of lamb?

- ☐ **A)** Venison
- ☐ **B)** Turkey
- ☐ **C)** Grouse
- ☐ **D)** Boar

24. What is the brand name of the Duke and Duchess of Sussex's audio production studio, non-profitable organization, and other multiplatform content-generation pursuits?

- ☐ **A)** Archetypes
- ☐ **B)** Archewell
- ☐ **C)** Archie's
- ☐ **D)** Archetypal

25. How was Prince Philip's coffin transported?

- ☐ **A)** By a horse-drawn carriage
- ☐ **B)** By a motorized hearse
- ☐ **C)** By a modified Land Rover
- ☐ **D)** On foot by pallbearers

A. 225

14. British Exceptionalism

You can't go far in the UK without a reminder that, for a time, Britain was the most powerful nation on earth. The British empire began in the late 1500s under Queen Elizabeth I, in a concerted effort to gain wealth and power (at least, more wealth and power than Spain) and spread Christianity and British ways of life.

Britain turned out to be very good at spreading its laws and customs to far-flung foreign places – not least because it was prepared to use force. Over nearly 400 years, the British empire spread from the Americas to take in colonies in Africa, Asia and Australasia. This was a bloody, violent process, made possible only by the slave trade.

By 1913, Britain ruled over 400 million people, making it the largest empire ever in history. Countries that were part of the empire in many ways benefited from its wealth, technological innovation and global reach – but invariably at a huge cost to their own culture and ways of life. The impact of this is still keenly felt today, with the empire dissolved only in the latter half of the twentieth century.

Countries that had treasures looted by the British are still lobbying for their return. Indigenous people are grappling with the loss of intergenerational wealth, language and lives. Even in Commonwealth countries that continue to observe an agreement with Britain, the legacy of empire is complex and close to the surface.

Meanwhile, in the former 'mother country', opinion is often

split between uncritical, unapologetic nostalgia for the glory days of Britannia's rule and the view that imperial rule was defined by state-sanctioned, racialized violence and slaughter.

In recent years, the reckoning over our national past and its relation to the present has been especially fraught, with statues of slavers torn down and protests over the legacy of empire. Even institutions like Kew Gardens have struggled to tread the line in recognizing its legacy of 'imperial botany'.

The fact is that we will likely never come to a consensus on whether the British empire was good or bad. But we can certainly strive to stick to the facts – as confronting, disturbing, ground-breaking and gobsmacking as they may be.

A. 228

Questions

1. Now, Britain's population is just over 67 million, but at its peak, what was the population of the empire?

□ **A)** 531 million

□ **B)** 200 million

□ **C)** 100 million

□ **D)** 450 million

2. . . . and, approximately, how much of the world's total landmass did the British empire cover?

□ **A)** 15 per cent

□ **B)** A quarter

□ **C)** A third

□ **D)** A half

3. What did Foreign Secretary Ernest Bevin request to be imprinted with 'the bloody Union Jack' as a matter of national prestige and security?

□ **A)** His ministerial 'red box'

□ **B)** Banknotes

□ **C)** The 1947 Dunkirk Treaty with France that he negotiated

□ **D)** The atomic bomb

4. What approximate share of UK adults can speak more than one language fluently?

- ☐ **A)** 33 per cent
- ☐ **B)** 15 per cent
- ☐ **C)** 25 per cent
- ☐ **D)** 50 per cent

5. In his strident declaration of post-empire optimism delivered in 1965, where did prime minister Harold Wilson declare Britain's 'frontiers'?

- ☐ **A)** The Himalayas
- ☐ **B)** The Moon
- ☐ **C)** The Arctic Circle
- ☐ **D)** The Mariana Trench

6. Which 'dominion' of the British empire was NOT granted independence and equal status within the Commonwealth under the Balfour Declaration of 1926?

- ☐ **A)** New Zealand
- ☐ **B)** Australia
- ☐ **C)** Canada
- ☐ **D)** India

7. What, in 1854, was made compulsory for the European troops of the East India Company's Bombay unit?

- ☐ **A)** A spouse
- ☐ **B)** A daily gin and tonic to prevent malaria
- ☐ **C)** Private security
- ☐ **D)** Facial hair

8. David Cameron got this wrong on *Letterman*: which composer, born 1710, wrote the music to 'Rule Britannia'?

☐ **A)** Thomas Arne
☐ **B)** Thomas Attwood
☐ **C)** Jonathan Battishill
☐ **D)** Charles Jennens

9. Who became the first recorded navigator to cross the Antarctic Circle?

☐ **A)** James Clark Ross
☐ **B)** Robert Falcon Scott
☐ **C)** James Cook
☐ **D)** Ernest Shackleton

10. The expedition by the British Navy's HMS *Challenger* between December 1872 and May 1876 was a crucial scientific voyage for what discipline in particular?

☐ **A)** Meteorology
☐ **B)** Oceanography
☐ **C)** Astronomy
☐ **D)** Biology

11. What are halyard, short drag, capstan and pumping all types of?

☐ **A)** Sea shanties
☐ **B)** Maritime knots
☐ **C)** Pipes for tobacco
☐ **D)** Teapots

12. Which of the below countries does NOT follow Greenwich Mean Time as standard all year round?

□ **A)** Iceland

□ **B)** Senegal

□ **C)** Guinea-Bissau

□ **D)** Belgium

13. What unusual essential is the royal family said to always travel with?

□ **A)** Mace spray

□ **B)** Bags of their own blood

□ **C)** A personal alarm

□ **D)** A direct relative

14. What was the largest mass migration ever?

□ **A)** Resettlement of Europe after Soviet Rule

□ **B)** Brexit

□ **C)** Partition in British India

□ **D)** The California Gold Rush from 1848–1850

15. Which celebrity chef's catchphrase has its roots in empire?

□ **A)** 'Buttery biscuit base'

□ **B)** 'Microwavé'

□ **C)** 'Pukka'

□ **D)** 'It's raw'

16. The Cullinan I diamond is mounted in the Sovereign's Sceptre with Cross, which King Charles carried at the coronation. Which country is calling for its return?

    ☐ **A)** South Africa

    ☐ **B)** India

    ☐ **C)** Pakistan

    ☐ **D)** Egypt

17. In 2019, Windsor Castle employed a fendersmith named Jones (a second-generation one, no less). What does he do, which his father also did before him?

    ☐ **A)** Make anvils and hammers for blacksmiths

    ☐ **B)** Craft wooden chests for household use

    ☐ **C)** Make metal buckles for shoes

    ☐ **D)** Maintain fireplaces and build and tend fires

18. Which countries became the fifty-fifth and fifty-sixth members of the Commonwealth in 2022?

    ☐ **A)** Rwanda and Togo

    ☐ **B)** Gabon and Togo

    ☐ **C)** Mozambique and Cameroon

    ☐ **D)** Antigua and Barbuda

19. The British East India Company took the Koh-i-Noor diamond from Duleep Singh in 1848, along with his power, his other property and his land. What did the maharaja, then still a young boy, receive in return?

    ☐ **A)** A role within the British India Company

    ☐ **B)** British sweets

    ☐ **C)** A life pension

    ☐ **D)** Nothing

20. Which of the below countries has NOT argued a claim to the Koh-i-Noor diamond?

☐ **A)** Pakistan

☐ **B)** Afghanistan

☐ **C)** Iran

☐ **D)** China

21. Name a British colony that was developed by a chartered company.

☐ **A)** Virginia

☐ **B)** New York

☐ **C)** Barbados

☐ **D)** India

22. The slave trade in the British empire was outlawed with the Slave Trade Act of 1807, and in Britain in 1834. Who was paid millions of pounds in compensation? A. 228

☐ **A)** Slave traders

☐ **B)** Slave owners

☐ **C)** Enslaved peoples

☐ **D)** Foreign governments

23. The cost of abolishing slavery and these compensation payouts in 1833 amounted to 40 per cent of the UK's national budget. When did the government finally pay off the debt?

☐ **A)** 1908

☐ **B)** 1933

☐ **C)** 1983

☐ **D)** 2015

24. Which Caribbean country removed Queen Elizabeth II as head of state in November 2021?

    ☐ **A)** Grenada

    ☐ **B)** Jamaica

    ☐ **C)** Barbados

    ☐ **D)** St Lucia

25. How much of the British Museum's collection is generally in storage at any given moment?

    ☐ **A)** 99 per cent

    ☐ **B)** 75 per cent

    ☐ **C)** 50 per cent

    ☐ **D)** 30 per cent

A. 228

15. Animals and Pets

According to the stereotype, we Brits are famously reserved – so much so that to disclose that we love our mums would be seen as an unforgivable slip of the stiff upper lip. The single exception to this, however – the one part of life where we can feel free to go all gooey and make ourselves vulnerable, without fear of exposure or ridicule – is animals.

Britons love animals. Even the right-wing press – invariably hostile to refugees fleeing war zones – will rally behind a four-legged friend in need, throwing its collective might behind campaigns to save the elephants or a dog from being put down.

Pets, in particular, are a unifier. Like our national passion for sports and games, pets present us with a socially permissible, non-political way of indulging our desire for silliness, softness and connection – our 'inner child', as an American might have it. Indeed, apart from the weather, owning a dog is perhaps the only acceptable way to strike up a conversation with a stranger.

But whatever extraversion or friendliness we might be able to channel in the company of animals, preferential treatment is reserved for our pets. In Britain, pets are not just part of the family; they're quite often the head of the household. A 2022 survey by YouGov found that one in three Britons with cats or dogs considered themselves to be their pet's 'parent'. Often the four-legged children enjoy more freedoms and affection than the two-legged ones.

It's a fact of life in the UK that's worth remembering, especially if you're not a particular animal person yourself: don't tell anyone.

A. 231

Questions

1. The Suffolk Punch is a breed of which animal?

- ☐ **A)** Horse
- ☐ **B)** Cow
- ☐ **C)** Sheep
- ☐ **D)** Duck

2. Which is the biggest of these mustelids?

- ☐ **A)** Polecat
- ☐ **B)** Pine marten
- ☐ **C)** Weasel
- ☐ **D)** Stoat

3. Before there were cockapoos, there were dorgis, a 'designer dog' breed developed by Queen Elizabeth II. But what was the cross with the corgi?

- ☐ **A)** Dachshund
- ☐ **B)** Dalmatian
- ☐ **C)** Dandie dinmont terrier
- ☐ **D)** Doberman

4. What made Geronimo the alpaca a cause célèbre of the tabloid press and self-appointed 'alpaca angels' in 2021?

☐ **A)** His apparent resemblance to Jeremy Corbyn

☐ **B)** Spitting on Piers Morgan during a television event

☐ **C)** Being a victim of bovine tuberculosis

☐ **D)** His amusing appearance on *This Morning*

5. Which of the below is NOT a real breed of cat originating from the UK?

☐ **A)** British shorthair

☐ **B)** Scottish fold

☐ **C)** Cornish Rex

☐ **D)** Manx

6. What did Charles Darwin, in a note to self written in 1838, reason was 'better than a dog anyhow'?

☐ **A)** Finches

☐ **B)** Children

☐ **C)** A giant tortoise

☐ **D)** A wife

7. What was the title of David Attenborough's first major television show as presenter?

☐ **A)** *Coelacanth*

☐ **B)** *Zoo Quest*

☐ **C)** *Animal, Vegetable, Mineral?*

☐ **D)** *Life on Air*

8. What did British zoologist Arthur Everett Shipley describe as 'one of the most beautiful of animals' in 1914?

- ☐ **A)** Emperor tamarin
- ☐ **B)** Pangolin
- ☐ **C)** Leech
- ☐ **D)** Platypus

9. 'A dog is for life, not just for Christmas' is the famous slogan of the Dogs' Trust. But what was the charity's name before that?

- ☐ **A)** National Canine Defence League
- ☐ **B)** Royal Society for the Protection of Dogs
- ☐ **C)** Canid Cross
- ☐ **D)** Blue Dogs

10. According to a 2019 survey, what percentage of Brits love their pet more than they love their partner?

- ☐ **A)** 5 per cent
- ☐ **B)** 9 per cent
- ☐ **C)** 15 per cent
- ☐ **D)** 25 per cent

11. In 1933, Virginia Woolf wrote an experimental novel from the perspective of an animal. But which animal?

- ☐ **A)** A seagull
- ☐ **B)** A spaniel
- ☐ **C)** A fly
- ☐ **D)** A horse

12. Welsh corgis and Cardigan corgis are technically different. How?

    ☐ **A)** One has a long tail, the other a short tail

    ☐ **B)** One is tan, one is dark brown

    ☐ **C)** Their countries of origin

    ☐ **D)** Cardigan corgis are only those dogs bred by the queen

13. Sir David Attenborough is the namesake of many species of animal. Which one of the below does NOT have a variety named after him?

    ☐ **A)** Snail

    ☐ **B)** Ant

    ☐ **C)** Weevil

    ☐ **D)** Shrimp

14. What type of animal is a slow-worm?

    ☐ **A)** Snake

    ☐ **B)** Lizard

    ☐ **C)** Worm

    ☐ **D)** Insect

15. In 1850 a specimen of desert snail on display at the British Museum caused a stir four years after first being displayed. Why?

    ☐ **A)** It was actually a previously undiscovered species

    ☐ **B)** It was found to still be alive

    ☐ **C)** It was claimed by Egypt as a national treasure

    ☐ **D)** It was still growing, post-death

16. What species of animal will be reintroduced to Ealing, London, in 2023?

    ☐ **A)** Beaver

    ☐ **B)** Pine marten

    ☐ **C)** Lynx

    ☐ **D)** Eagle owl

17. Larry the cat has lived at 10 Downing Street since 2011 and has served under five prime ministers. What is his formal title?

    ☐ **A)** Purr Minister

    ☐ **B)** Minister for Milk

    ☐ **C)** Chief Mouser to the Cabinet Office

    ☐ **D)** Member of Purrliament

18. What inspired Hugh Lofting to write the charming Doctor Dolittle stories?

    ☐ **A)** The horrors of war

    ☐ **B)** The real-life news story of a man who claimed to communicate with animals

    ☐ **C)** Lofting's thwarted ambition to be a naturalist

    ☐ **D)** An encounter with a charismatic parrot

19. In 1995 prime minister John Major made headlines for his reported neglect of what pet?

    ☐ **A)** Hamster

    ☐ **B)** Tortoise

    ☐ **C)** Dog

    ☐ **D)** Goldfish

20. What was the name of the dog on the Australian soap opera *Neighbours*?

- ☐ **A)** Bouncer
- ☐ **B)** Wellard
- ☐ **C)** Oliver
- ☐ **D)** Toadie

21. Which of the following is NOT a species of British butterfly?

- ☐ **A)** High brown fritillary
- ☐ **B)** Holly blue
- ☐ **C)** White-letter hairstreak
- ☐ **D)** Rainbow skipper

22. Why were hedgehogs prized in Victorian kitchens?

- ☐ **A)** Servants used to race them for money
- ☐ **B)** They made a delicious stew
- ☐ **C)** They kept the black beetles away
- ☐ **D)** They were the basis for a popular children's game

23. Complete P. G. Wodehouse's theory of life: 'All you need is about two real friends, a regular supply of books, and a . . .'

- ☐ **A)** Pug
- ☐ **B)** Peke
- ☐ **C)** Persian cat
- ☐ **D)** Poodle

24. Crufts is one of the most famous dog shows in the world, with its own tradition of scandals, from protests to poisonings. What happened in 2010?

    ☐ **A)** A streaker disrupted the gundog judging

    ☐ **B)** A fire alarm forced an evacuation of the arena, with 20,000-odd dogs

    ☐ **C)** The terrier group winner was accused of having forged papers

    ☐ **D)** A protestor stormed Best in Show on behalf of mixed breeds

25. Which hit pop song was supposedly written about Noel Fitzpatrick, aka 'The Supervet'?

    ☐ **A)** 'Little Lion Man' by Mumford and Sons

    ☐ **B)** 'Animals' by Maroon 5

    ☐ **C)** 'Cowboy Casanova' by Carrie Underwood

    ☐ **D)** 'Toxic' by Britney Spears

A- 231

16. Transport

Like the weather, the subject of transportation presents a wealth of conversational possibilities and potential intrigue for Brits. It's comfortable common ground: something that we have all had experience of, perhaps even in the recent past, and which we can talk about freely without risk of revealing anything too personal, like who we vote for, or what our surname is.

'Have you travelled far?', for instance, is a fantastic opener because it manages to package up at once personal, factual and neutral enquiries into one polite, pithy question. You might soon find yourself in a lively debate on the merits of the M1 versus the M12, or a mutual commiseration over the delays on the Overground.

And if the chat is really flying, the subject of transport may even open up avenues for a discussion of the weather, and vice versa – meaning you're on safe conversational territory for at least the next twenty minutes, without having to get anything near so personal as their work or – God forbid – their relationship status.

The other bonus of talking about buses, trains and automobiles is that it gives Britons a chance to indirectly reflect on their past innovation. The British railways are the result of visionary leadership in government that centred on the needs of the people. The Tube is a Victorian-era underground network that not only still functions but is widely used.

It does allow for an element of national pride. When you talk about which route you took to your destination, and how well or otherwise it served you, you are actually talking about problems that Britons have been navigating for hundreds of years.

You're on safe ground, talking about transport. You might even learn a useful shortcut.

A. 233

Questions

1. In 2008, then London mayor Boris Johnson outlawed drinking on the Tube, prompting one last party to be organized on Facebook. On which line was it held?

□ **A)** The Victoria Line

□ **B)** The Circle Line

□ **C)** The Northern Line

□ **D)** The District Line

2. Which TfL station is on the site of a seventeenth-century plague pit?

□ **A)** Aldgate

□ **B)** Monument

□ **C)** Charing Cross

□ **D)** Moorgate

3. Which of the following is NOT one of the bridges over the Thames?

□ **A)** Lambeth Bridge

□ **B)** Millennium Bridge

□ **C)** Garden Bridge

□ **D)** Kew Bridge

4. What were British cyclists required to do until 1930?

- ☐ **A)** Wear a helmet
- ☐ **B)** Wear appropriate cycling shoes
- ☐ **C)** Ring the bell continuously
- ☐ **D)** Verbally indicate turns

5. Which London airport is the opening scene of *Love Actually* filmed in?

- ☐ **A)** Heathrow
- ☐ **B)** Stansted
- ☐ **C)** City
- ☐ **D)** Gatwick

6. Smoking on trains and in train stations was banned in which year?

- ☐ **A)** 1975
- ☐ **B)** 1987
- ☐ **C)** 1998
- ☐ **D)** 2000

7. How is Isambard Kingdom Brunel said to have designed the two-mile Box Tunnel, near Bath?

- ☐ **A)** So the sun shone through it on the morning of his birthday
- ☐ **B)** To set a new record for the world's longest railway tunnel
- ☐ **C)** For use as a bunker or armoury in the event of war
- ☐ **D)** To extend the London to Bath road

8. How many babies have been born on the Tube?

- [ ] **A)** 98
- [ ] **B)** 34
- [ ] **C)** 20
- [ ] **D)** 3

9. Roughly 475,000 planes pass through Heathrow each year. A plane lands or takes off every:

- [ ] **A)** 10 seconds
- [ ] **B)** 45 seconds
- [ ] **C)** 60 seconds
- [ ] **D)** 90 seconds

10. Where was Britain's first roundabout built in 1907?

- [ ] **A)** Dorchester
- [ ] **B)** Letchworth Garden City
- [ ] **C)** Leicester
- [ ] **D)** Redditch

11. The longest train journey in the UK is from Penzance to Aberdeen. How long does it take?

- [ ] **A)** 13.5 hours
- [ ] **B)** 10 hours
- [ ] **C)** 20 hours
- [ ] **D)** 15 hours

12. What did the Harland & Wolff factory in East Belfast make?

- ☐ **A)** Engines
- ☐ **B)** Cars
- ☐ **C)** Ships
- ☐ **D)** Locomotives

13. How long does it take to walk, on average, the length of the Thames, from the Cotswolds to Woolwich?

- ☐ **A)** 5–7 days
- ☐ **B)** 8–10 days
- ☐ **C)** 12–14 days
- ☐ **D)** 16–18 days

14. Why was Heathrow's Terminal One closed?

- ☐ **A)** Damage during the war
- ☐ **B)** Superstitions
- ☐ **C)** To make room for Terminal Two
- ☐ **D)** Electrical fire

15. In 2021, what was the average time it took Brits to travel to work?

- ☐ **A)** 23 minutes
- ☐ **B)** 28 minutes
- ☐ **C)** 35 minutes
- ☐ **D)** 47 minutes

16. 81 per cent of this region's population travels to work by car, the highest percentage of the UK by 2 per cent. Which region?

- ☐ **A)** The south-east
- ☐ **B)** Yorkshire
- ☐ **C)** East of England
- ☐ **D)** West Midlands

17. How far can you travel by Tube without changing trains?

- ☐ **A)** 5.5 miles
- ☐ **B)** 27.9 miles
- ☐ **C)** 34.1 miles
- ☐ **D)** 37.8 miles

18. The average train speed on the Tube is

- ☐ **A)** 12.4mph
- ☐ **B)** 15.5mph
- ☐ **C)** 20.5mph
- ☐ **D)** 23mph

19. The British Airways motto is

- ☐ **A)** 'To fly, to serve'
- ☐ **B)** 'Together we go places'
- ☐ **C)** 'Flying is magic'
- ☐ **D)** 'Flying, together'

20. The inflight British Airways magazine, available in all classes, is called:

- ☐ **A)** *Highlight*
- ☐ **B)** *High Life*
- ☐ **C)** *High Society*
- ☐ **D)** *Flying High*

21. What does the P&O in P&O Ferries stand for?

- ☐ **A)** Polar and Ontario
- ☐ **B)** Philip and Olson
- ☐ **C)** Polaris and Offshore
- ☐ **D)** Peninsular and Oriental

22. What was the name of the first P&O ship?

- ☐ **A)** *William Fawcett*
- ☐ **B)** *Neptune*
- ☐ **C)** *Princess Royal*
- ☐ **D)** *Robert Scott*

23. Which of these is NOT the name of a naval ship at the 1805 Battle of Trafalgar?

- ☐ **A)** *Orion*
- ☐ **B)** *Naiad*
- ☐ **C)** *Sirius*
- ☐ **D)** *Hercules*

24. Which monarch is responsible for building up the English Royal Navy to combat the Spanish Armada?

- ☐ **A)** Edward VI
- ☐ **B)** Henry VIII
- ☐ **C)** Elizabeth I
- ☐ **D)** James VI

25. At 603 metres, the longest unbroken train station in the UK is:

- ☐ **A)** Gloucester
- ☐ **B)** Cambridge
- ☐ **C)** Leeds
- ☐ **D)** Norwich

A. 233

17. Brexit

23 June 2016: a momentous date. Regardless of which side of the vote you came down on, you might well consider recent British history as split between BB and AB: Before Brexit and After Brexit. Households were divided over the issue, often but not always along generational lines. Relationships were tested, and some actually split up.

Rarely have Britons been faced with a political issue so live, so fundamental to who we are as a nation or so actively contested in our homes. Nor have we seen a debate drag on for so long.

Between the referendum going into Parliament in May 2015 and Britain actually leaving the European Union, we will soon have collectively been navigating Brexit for a full ten years. That's a decade of circular back-and-forth about Dover, the Irish back-stop, slogans on big buses.

Often it has seemed less like a trade negotiation and more like a bureaucratic form of torture – not least for the poor souls tasked with 'getting it done'.

Now that we have finally severed our forty-year union, you might like to put Brexit behind you. But, as with ending any long relationship, moving on is hard. Reminders are everywhere, in the queues at the airport or the empty shelves at the supermarket.

What Britain will be without Europe is yet to be seen. For now, why not relive the memories?

A. 235

Questions

1. The vote in favour of Brexit was in June 2016. How long did it take for Britain to finally leave the EU?

    ☐ **A)** 3.5 years

    ☐ **B)** 4 years

    ☐ **C)** 3 years

    ☐ **D)** 2.5 years

2. The UK notified the European Council of its intention to leave the EU on 29 March 2019. How many extensions to the Article 50 deadline were granted by the European Council?

    ☐ **A)** 1

    ☐ **B)** 3

    ☐ **C)** 5

    ☐ **D)** 6

3. In just one of many lively terms in its 'Glossary of Brexit', how did the House of Commons library characterize the first Article 50 extension?

    ☐ **A)** 'Managed no-deal'

    ☐ **B)** 'Slow Brexit'

    ☐ **C)** 'Freedom to move'

    ☐ **D)** 'Flextension'

4. In January 2021, what did Commons leader Jacob Rees-Mogg claim were 'better and happier' post-Brexit, prompting the speaker Sir Lindsay Hoyle to intervene?

- ☐ **A)** Nurses
- ☐ **B)** Livestock
- ☐ **C)** Farmers
- ☐ **D)** Fish

5. How much was the UK's EU 'divorce bill' initially estimated to be?

- ☐ **A)** £5 billion
- ☐ **B)** £15 billion
- ☐ **C)** £39 billion
- ☐ **D)** £50 billion

6. What is the name of the pro-Remain guerrilla campaign group that seeks to remind the public of the government's failures?

- ☐ **A)** Led by Donkeys
- ☐ **B)** Thick as Pigs
- ☐ **C)** Behaving like Animals
- ☐ **D)** Chickens Out

7. Where did the European Banking Authority transfer its headquarters after the UK referendum?

- ☐ **A)** Paris
- ☐ **B)** Antwerp
- ☐ **C)** Brussels
- ☐ **D)** Amsterdam

8. What share of Scottish voters in the referendum opted for Remain?

    ☐ **A)** 52 per cent

    ☐ **B)** 62 per cent

    ☐ **C)** 72 per cent

    ☐ **D)** 82 per cent

9. Who was appointed the EU's chief negotiator?

    ☐ **A)** Jean-Claude Juncker

    ☐ **B)** Donald Tusk

    ☐ **C)** Michel Barnier

    ☐ **D)** Sophie Wilmès

10. How much money was promised to the NHS, on the side of the Vote Leave campaign bus?

    ☐ **A)** £35 million a day

    ☐ **B)** £350 million a week

    ☐ **C)** £350 million a year

    ☐ **D)** £350 million total

11. 'Take Back Control' was the Vote Leave campaign's slogan. What was the slogan for the Remain campaign?

    ☐ **A)** 'Stronger, Safer and Better Off'

    ☐ **B)** 'We Are Europe'

    ☐ **C)** 'Safer In'

    ☐ **D)** 'Better Together'

12. Who said a free trade agreement with the EU should be 'one of the easiest in human history'?

- ☐ **A)** Liam Fox
- ☐ **B)** Jacob Rees-Mogg
- ☐ **C)** Michael Gove
- ☐ **D)** David Davis

13. Bananas were an oft-repeated sticking point. What in particular was the EU said to be concerned with?

- ☐ **A)** Their size
- ☐ **B)** Their curve
- ☐ **C)** Their colour
- ☐ **D)** Their country of origin

14. Which country did the Vote Leave campaign heavily suggest would soon be joining the EU, despite the objections of EU members?

- ☐ **A)** Turkey
- ☐ **B)** Albania
- ☐ **C)** Serbia
- ☐ **D)** Moldova

15. When did the UK join the European Union in the first place?

- ☐ **A)** 1961
- ☐ **B)** 1967
- ☐ **C)** 1973
- ☐ **D)** 1976

16. Which other countries have withdrawn from the EU in its history?

    ☐ **A)** Only the UK

    ☐ **B)** French Algeria

    ☐ **C)** Greenland

    ☐ **D)** Saint Pierre and Miquelon

17. By what means did UKIP candidate David Moreland claim, in November 2019, immigrants were illegally entering the UK?

    ☐ **A)** Submarines

    ☐ **B)** Paragliding

    ☐ **C)** Scuba diving

    ☐ **D)** Swimming

18. Announced in February 2023, what is the new name of the post-Brexit legal agreement relating to goods crossing the Irish Sea from Great Britain to Northern Ireland?

    ☐ **A)** The Fairmont Framework

    ☐ **B)** The Northern Ireland Protocol

    ☐ **C)** The New Northern Ireland Protocol

    ☐ **D)** The Windsor Framework

19. Which musician admitted to 'immediately' applying for an Irish passport after the referendum result?

    ☐ **A)** Noel Gallagher

    ☐ **B)** Morrissey

    ☐ **C)** Mick Jagger

    ☐ **D)** Jarvis Cocker

20. After seven years, what impact has Brexit had on inward immigration?

- ☐ **A)** Decreased minimally
- ☐ **B)** Increased substantially
- ☐ **C)** Decreased substantially
- ☐ **D)** No substantial change

21. As of May 2023, the United Kingdom has thirty-six active free trade agreements with nations and trade blocs, covering ninety-eight countries and territories. How many are new post-Brexit?

- ☐ **A)** 3
- ☐ **B)** 11
- ☐ **C)** 14
- ☐ **D)** 29

22. In a now-infamous 2015 tweet, then prime minister David Cameron said Britain faced a 'simple and inescapable choice': 'stability and strong government' with him – or, what?

- ☐ **A)** 'Threat of deficits'
- ☐ **B)** 'Debt and disorder'
- ☐ **C)** 'Chaos with Ed Miliband'
- ☐ **D)** 'Losing Labour'

23. In a 2023 YouGov poll, how many respondents said leaving the EU had been the wrong call?

- ☐ **A)** 74 per cent
- ☐ **B)** 68 per cent
- ☐ **C)** 53 per cent
- ☐ **D)** 42 per cent

24. In April 2018, Amber Rudd claimed that the registration process for EU citizens living in the UK post-Brexit would be 'as easy as shopping at' which affordable luxury store?

☐ **A)** Jigsaw

☐ **B)** L. K. Bennett

☐ **C)** Reiss

☐ **D)** Russell & Bromley

25. Shortly before the Brexit vote, Boris Johnson accused the EU of trying to create a political superstate, just like – who?

☐ **A)** The Romans

☐ **B)** Napoleon

☐ **C)** Hitler and the Nazis

☐ **D)** All of the above

A. 235

18. Etiquette and Customs

All right, enough messing around with history and politics: if you really want to get on in Great Britain, this is the only bit of the quiz that matters.

One of the facts of life in the UK which few people will ever tell you is that you can know all of the important dates, the names of the monarchs and key passages from the classics of literature, but if you mispronounce a single word the jig is up: you've marked yourself out as not belonging.

That's one theory why there are those place names like Salisbury and Durham, which seemed designed to trip you up. ('Salz-bree' and 'Durrum', just FYI.) How you speak, from your accent to your choice of words, is widely understood as a signifier of your standing in society.

Of course, these tests are arbitrary. That's the point – they don't really matter, which is what makes them such effective tests. The English in particular can be like undercover detectives, highly attuned to clues such as what kind of car you drive, what you call the midday meal, and – the smoking gun – what school you went to.

How much money you have is only a part of it. The central importance of class to British society is why people pay thousands to send their children to private schools when a perfectly serviceable education can often be had for free or close to it – for the access, opportunities and polished finish that come from learning alongside the elite.

The UK is not a meritocracy: those who fare the best tend to have been handed an advantage. The good news is, just like history and the complete works of Dickens, you can scrub up on the important bits on your own for free on Google.

A. 239

Questions

1. How was the 'predominantly white' rule for players' dress at Wimbledon clarified in 1995?

    ☐ **A)** 'Off-white and cream allowed'

    ☐ **B)** 'Exclusively white'

    ☐ **C)** 'Only white'

    ☐ **D)** 'Almost entirely white'

2. When and why is St Totteringham celebrated?

    ☐ **A)** The first day of the Premier League season

    ☐ **B)** The end of the transfer window

    ☐ **C)** When it becomes impossible for Tottenham to finish above Arsenal

    ☐ **D)** The last workday before the Euros

3. What is believed to be the most common pub name in the UK?

    ☐ **A)** The Red Lion

    ☐ **B)** The White Horse

    ☐ **C)** The Rose

    ☐ **D)** The Royal Oak

4. What is the most common street name in Great Britain?

☐ **A)** Station Road

☐ **B)** High Street

☐ **C)** Main Road

☐ **D)** Church Road

5. Among football players, what is 'getting the hairdryer treatment' euphemistic for?

☐ **A)** Being abused on the pitch by the opposing side

☐ **B)** Being puffed up and glamorized by the press

☐ **C)** Expecting preferential treatment as a result of a swollen ego

☐ **D)** Receiving an angry telling-off from their manager

6. Which country was the first to ban smoking in enclosed public spaces?

☐ **A)** England

☐ **B)** Wales

☐ **C)** Northern Ireland

☐ **D)** Scotland

7. Ed Sheeran's 'Galway Girl' namechecks the céilí: a traditional Irish social gathering. Which of the below is the correct spelling of the equivalent word in Scots Gaelic?

☐ **A)** Cèilidh

☐ **B)** Cailidh

☐ **C)** Céilidh

☐ **D)** Cailidh

8. What derives from the pagan tradition monandaeg?

☐ **A)** The month of November

☐ **B)** The days of the week

☐ **C)** New Year's Eve

☐ **D)** Hallowe'en

9. Which of these is NOT a real law?

☐ **A)** You may not walk a cow down the street in daylight

☐ **B)** You may not be found drunk in a pub

☐ **C)** You may not fly a kite in public

☐ **D)** You may not leave a dog in the driver's seat of a vehicle, even if it's parked

10. In Victorian England, what were considered appropriate visiting hours for a lady?

☐ **A)** Before noon

☐ **B)** Between noon and 3 p.m.

☐ **C)** Between 3 p.m. and 5 p.m.

☐ **D)** After 5 p.m.

11. In 2002, what were police officers wanting to join the Met's Special Branch tested on to ensure their 'broad-based knowledge'?

☐ **A)** *Teletubbies*

☐ **B)** *Big Brother*

☐ **C)** S-Club 7

☐ **D)** The *X-Factor* judges

12. Which Victorian Brit co-founded the 'Glutton Club', dedicated to experimenting with cooking exotic animals and consuming meat 'before unknown to the human palate'?

    ☐ **A)** Charles Dickens

    ☐ **B)** Charles Darwin

    ☐ **C)** Oscar Wilde

    ☐ **D)** Thomas Hardy

13. What custom did Queen Victoria popularize?

    ☐ **A)** White wedding dresses

    ☐ **B)** Mourning black

    ☐ **C)** Nicknames

    ☐ **D)** Marriage between cousins

14. What is the 'proper' way to stir tea?

    ☐ **A)** Clockwise

    ☐ **B)** Counterclockwise

    ☐ **C)** Up and down

    ☐ **D)** With your pinkie finger sticking out

15. What is the maximum age you can be called for jury service in the UK?

    ☐ **A)** 60

    ☐ **B)** 65

    ☐ **C)** 70

    ☐ **D)** None of the above

16. What was the world's first Sunday newspaper?

☐ **A)** *Sunday Times*

☐ **B)** *Sunday Express*

☐ **C)** *Observer*

☐ **D)** *Sunday Independent*

17. What fourteenth-century European trend was initially derided by the very manly British as a 'feminine affectation'?

☐ **A)** Wine glasses

☐ **B)** Aprons

☐ **C)** Napkins

☐ **D)** Forks

18. At the start of the First World War, tanks were grouped according to their 'gender', because of course they were. What distinguished the 'female' tanks from the 'male' ones?

☐ **A)** The 'females' carried machine guns, while the 'males' had cannons attached

☐ **B)** There was no difference; it was administrative

☐ **C)** The 'female' tanks had more comfortable interiors

☐ **D)** The 'female' tanks were lighter

19. What is the popular name of the Greenwich Time Signal?

☐ **A)** The pip-pips

☐ **B)** The pips

☐ **C)** The toodlepips

☐ **D)** The nips

20. Where, according to a 1642 law, can the reigning monarch NOT set foot in England?

□ **A)** Edinburgh Castle

□ **B)** Stonehenge

□ **C)** The House of Commons

□ **D)** The entire City of London

21. *Love Island* has transformed the way Britons talk – especially about people they do or don't want to shag. What is 'the ick'?

□ **A)** Something you would never dream of eating

□ **B)** Something revolting found or observed on a loved one's body

□ **C)** An insult to describe someone who's gone soft

□ **D)** An abrupt and often terminal reversal in attraction to a partner

22. According to a 2017 YouGov analysis of more than 42,000 Brits, what do most people in England call the main evening meal?

□ **A)** Dinner

□ **B)** Tea

□ **C)** Supper

□ **D)** Don't know

23. What percentage of the British population is privately educated?

□ **A)** 7 per cent

□ **B)** 14 per cent

□ **C)** 17 per cent

□ **D)** 22 per cent

24. What was the 'Tebbit test' proposed by Tory MP Norman Tebbit in 1990, sparking outrage and debate? (To be clear: all the possibilities were explored by Tebbit at some point or another, but only one became known as the 'Tebbit test'.)

    ☐ **A)** Whether aid for Africa helped the poor or went towards 'guns for warlords'

    ☐ **B)** Whether homosexuals could be considered fit to be Home Secretary

    ☐ **C)** Whether British Asians who supported their country of ancestry in cricket against England could actually be considered British

    ☐ **D)** Whether same-sex marriage laws could one day enable a future monarch to marry his own son and so escape inheritance tax

25. William Pitt the Elder, prime minister between 1766 and 1768, declared that it was 'better to smile than to' – what?

    ☐ **A)** Speak in haste

    ☐ **B)** Cry

    ☐ **C)** Look back in anger

    ☐ **D)** Laugh out loud

A. 239

19. The Other Countries

Of course, we know that the 'United Kingdom' is a country consisting of England, Scotland, Wales and Northern Ireland, bringing together a long and often fraught history of conquest and conflict, union and division. And of course we know that, when we talk about 'Great Britain' and 'Brits', we are actually talking about the island landmass on which three of the four are situated, and the people that live there. We learned all of that at school.

But the truth is that this undeniably important nuance can sometimes be lost in casual conversation – and especially if we're in south-east England. Invariably, when we talk about 'Brits', we are talking about 'England' – and maybe even 'London'. You might say that, occasionally, the context is lacking.

There is nothing fundamentally 'British' about sausage rolls or marmalade: all national identity is to some extent a construct, and there is just as much that divides us as there is that unites us. Nonetheless, life on these isles is consistently reduced to a small and often privileged group of people, many of them with a pied-à-terre in Marylebone and a weekly newspaper column.

This narrow vision of 'Britishness' erases the distinct history, culture, politics and traditions of Scotland, Wales and Northern Ireland, whose centuries-old ties with England have been marked by intermittent conflict. Our union, after all, is not guaranteed; the vote for Scottish independence (and the high turnout against Brexit) was a reminder of this.

But what makes Britain great is the combination of its distinct constituent parts, as we'd do well to remember when we talk about 'life in the UK'. This isn't (only) England.

A. 243

Questions

1. What we know as the United Kingdom or Great Britain has evolved out of a series of agreements, separations and unions over centuries. When was the first signed?

    ☐ **A)** 1992

    ☐ **B)** 1808

    ☐ **C)** 1801

    ☐ **D)** 1707

2. A traditional 'boxty' might be one of the ingredients that distinguish a full Irish breakfast from a full English. What is it?

    ☐ **A)** A potato pancake

    ☐ **B)** A black pudding

    ☐ **C)** A white pudding (without blood)

    ☐ **D)** Soda bread

3. The 85 per cent turnout in the 2014 Scottish independence referendum was the highest recorded in the UK since the 1910 general election, which preceded the introduction of universal suffrage. The 'no's had it – but with what percentage of the vote?

    ☐ **A)** 51 per cent

    ☐ **B)** 55 per cent

    ☐ **C)** 57 per cent

    ☐ **D)** 61 per cent

4. The Cowal Games, held in Dunoon, are the largest Highland Games in Scotland – but where are the oldest held?

    ☐ **A)** Braemar

    ☐ **B)** Inverness

    ☐ **C)** Ceres

    ☐ **D)** Pitlochry

5. Robert Burns's poem, opening with 'Fair is your honest happy face', is addressed to and about what iconic emblem of Scotland?

    ☐ **A)** Haggis

    ☐ **B)** Shetland sheep

    ☐ **C)** The thistle

    ☐ **D)** Loch Ness

6. Wales is believed to have more of these per square mile than any other place in the world. What?

    ☐ **A)** Sheep

    ☐ **B)** Castles

    ☐ **C)** Mountains

    ☐ **D)** Pubs

7. Which Welsh soldier was credited with founding England's Tudor dynasty?

    ☐ **A)** Owen Tudor

    ☐ **B)** Henry Tudor

    ☐ **C)** Edward Tudor

    ☐ **D)** Dafydd Tudor

8. What historical event concludes *Derry Girls* season two?

☐ **A)** The 1986 Chernobyl disaster

☐ **B)** Bill Clinton's 1995 visit to Derry

☐ **C)** The 1998 Omagh bombing

☐ **D)** The 1994 ceasefire in the Irish Civil War

9. Which famous Welsh figure was raised in the town of Mumbles?

☐ **A)** Sir Anthony Hopkins

☐ **B)** Richard Burton

☐ **C)** Catherine Zeta-Jones

☐ **D)** Tom Jones

10. Which is the largest national park in Wales?

☐ **A)** The Brecon Beacons

☐ **B)** Pembrokeshire coast

☐ **C)** Snowdonia

☐ **D)** Cambrian Mountains

11. Who was the lead singer of Welsh band Catatonia?

☐ **A)** Jem

☐ **B)** Cerys Matthews

☐ **C)** Charlotte Church

☐ **D)** Christina Booth

12. Which Welsh city is considered the smallest in the UK?

☐ **A)** St Davids

☐ **B)** St Asaph

☐ **C)** Bangor

☐ **D)** Aberystwyth

13. How many characters are there in the UK's longest place name, located in Wales and often shortened to Llanfair PG?

- ☐ **A)** 38
- ☐ **B)** 47
- ☐ **C)** 58
- ☐ **D)** 70

14. According to legend, what did St David instruct Welsh soldiers to wear on their helmets in order to to identify themselves in battle against the Saxon invaders?

- ☐ **A)** Daffodils
- ☐ **B)** Leeks
- ☐ **C)** A red dragon insignia
- ☐ **D)** An oak-tree leaf

15. Named after the historic Welsh county, what are traditional Glamorgan sausages made of?

- ☐ **A)** Cheese
- ☐ **B)** Horse
- ☐ **C)** Chicken
- ☐ **D)** Wild boar

16. What approximate proportion of the Welsh population speaks Welsh daily?

- ☐ **A)** 5 per cent
- ☐ **B)** 10 per cent
- ☐ **C)** 15 per cent
- ☐ **D)** 20 per cent

17. The lion and the unicorn appear on the royal coat of arms. If the lion represents England, what does the unicorn represent?

☐ **A)** Scotland

☐ **B)** Wales

☐ **C)** Ireland

☐ **D)** The Commonwealth

18. What city was known as the 'second city of the British empire' and powered by the slave trade, as evinced by its present-day Jamaica Street, Antigua Street and Tobago Street?

☐ **A)** Cardiff

☐ **B)** Dublin

☐ **C)** Newport

☐ **D)** Glasgow

19. Which Scottish city is known as the 'Granite City'?

☐ **A)** Aberdeen

☐ **B)** Edinburgh

☐ **C)** Inverness

☐ **D)** Dundee

20. Tyrone is the largest of the six counties in Northern Ireland, but which is the smallest?

☐ **A)** Louth

☐ **B)** Carlow

☐ **C)** Cork

☐ **D)** Armagh

21. Who was the inaugural prime minister of Northern Ireland from 1921 to 1940?

    ☐ **A)** John Miller Andrews

    ☐ **B)** James Craig

    ☐ **C)** Basil Brooke

    ☐ **D)** Terence O'Neill

22. What is thought to be the most accurate English translation for 'Sinn Féin', from Irish?

    ☐ **A)** 'Ourselves' / 'We ourselves'

    ☐ **B)** 'Ourselves alone' / 'Solely us'

    ☐ **C)** 'Workers' party'

    ☐ **D)** 'We are all one here'

23. What is the name of the river that flows through Belfast?

    ☐ **A)** Boyne

    ☐ **B)** Shannon

    ☐ **C)** Lagan

    ☐ **D)** Foyle

24. Once widely found in County Fermanagh and County Tyrone, a greasy pippin is a variety of what?

    ☐ **A)** Apple

    ☐ **B)** Seabird

    ☐ **C)** Moss

    ☐ **D)** Wildflower

25. With which country was Scotland's Auld Alliance cemented in 1295?

    ☐ **A)** Germany

    ☐ **B)** England

    ☐ **C)** Norway

    ☐ **D)** France

A. 243

20. Brits Abroad

The days of empire may be over, but Britons remain active and high-profile participants on the world's stage. Just look at our constant holidaying.

Even after voting to withdraw from the European Union in 2016, making it more expensive for UK residents to travel abroad, the number of outbound tourist trips has been steadily on the rise. Britain may well be for the British – but it seems that we can't wait to get away ourselves every now and then.

If anything, the risk and disruptions brought about by the Covid-19 pandemic only fuelled our wanderlust. All told, UK residents made 71 million visits abroad in 2022, at a cost of a colossal £58.5 billion. The most common reason given was to see friends and relatives – itself proof of our far-flung ties.

Our presence abroad isn't always welcome, however. British tourists have a poor reputation in many popular destinations in Europe, reflecting our tendency to believe that what goes on offshore stays offshore. The bad behaviour often starts before we're even on the plane, with airport drinking considered a peculiarly English activity.

But, oddly, this coexists with the pride widely felt at Britain's international achievements. Whether it's Ed Sheeran and Adele climbing the US music charts or Team GB cleaning up at the Olympics, we love to measure our successes against those of other countries. If only we could decide if we're the plucky underdog or the time-honoured champion . . .

A. 246

Questions

1. Who was the first British artist or band to play at the Super Bowl halftime show?

    ☐ **A)** The Rolling Stones

    ☐ **B)** Paul McCartney

    ☐ **C)** Phil Collins

    ☐ **D)** Sting

2. The first ever international cricket game was held in 1844, but unbelievably did not feature any British team. Who was it between?

    ☐ **A)** Canada and the US

    ☐ **B)** New Zealand and Australia

    ☐ **C)** India and New Zealand

    ☐ **D)** South Africa and Australia

3. Over ten seasons of *Friends*, which of the below Brits did NOT make a cameo appearance?

    ☐ **A)** Sarah Ferguson

    ☐ **B)** Gary Oldman

    ☐ **C)** Robbie Coltrane

    ☐ **D)** Sir Richard Branson

4. The UK and Ireland make up the top two Guinness-drinking countries. But which is number three?

- [ ] **A)** Nigeria
- [ ] **B)** Malaysia
- [ ] **C)** The United States
- [ ] **D)** Cameroon

5. Wayne Rooney played for which American professional football – sorry, 'soccer' – club from 2018 to 2020?

- [ ] **A)** New York Bulls
- [ ] **B)** DC United
- [ ] **C)** LA Galaxy
- [ ] **D)** New York City

6. All of the below footballers were born outside the UK, but who is the only footballer ever to have played for England without having lived in the United Kingdom first?

- [ ] **A)** Tony Dorigo
- [ ] **B)** Richard Geaves
- [ ] **C)** William Bryant
- [ ] **D)** Owen Hargreaves

7. First described in 1997, what is Manhattanhenge, observed in New York twice a year?

- [ ] **A)** When the setting sun is framed by skyscrapers
- [ ] **B)** A gathering of New York-based Brits to mark the solstice
- [ ] **C)** A manmade replica of Stonehenge outside the Natural History Museum
- [ ] **D)** The first crop of skyscrapers to be built on Manhattan Island

8. According to Boris Johnson's Conservative Party conference speech in 2016 – described by journalist Sathnam Sanghera as 'the single most imperial pronouncement by any British politician in my lifetime' – how many people born in Britain now live abroad?

- ☐ **A)** One in five
- ☐ **B)** One in ten
- ☐ **C)** One in four
- ☐ **D)** One in twelve

9. 'The people of these islands are more movable than other nations, and large numbers of them are always abroad,' observed the compilers of the 1861 census. Between 1900 and 1914, roughly what share of the British population made a permanent move overseas?

- ☐ **A)** 1 per cent
- ☐ **B)** 5 per cent
- ☐ **C)** 7 per cent
- ☐ **D)** 12 per cent

10. Which country saw so much immigration from Cornwall in the latter half of the nineteenth century, it became known as 'Greater Cornwall'?

- ☐ **A)** South Africa
- ☐ **B)** Canada
- ☐ **C)** New Zealand
- ☐ **D)** Australia

11. English muffins were invented by Samuel Bath Thomas, an Englishman – but not in England. Where were his first so-called 'toaster crumpets' devised, in 1880?

☐ **A)** New York

☐ **B)** York, Western Australia

☐ **C)** York, Sierra Leone

☐ **D)** York, Ontario

12. Which Led Zeppelin song has been sampled by Eminem, the Beastie Boys and Beyoncé?

☐ **A)** 'Kashmir'

☐ **B)** 'When the Levee Breaks'

☐ **C)** 'Stairway to Heaven'

☐ **D)** 'Immigrant 2'

13. Which British female singer holds the record for most Grammy Awards won in a single ceremony?

☐ **A)** Annie Lennox

☐ **B)** Dua Lipa

☐ **C)** Amy Winehouse

☐ **D)** Adele

14. The acronym 'FILTH' is well established in City and legal circles to describe a certain section of its members. But what does it stand for?

☐ **A)** Fall In Love? Total Headache

☐ **B)** Failed In London, Try Hong Kong

☐ **C)** Feeling Lost? Try Hide

☐ **D)** Failed In Life, Now To Hell

15. Before becoming prime minister of Pakistan, Imran Khan played cricket for which English county?

- ☐ **A)** Warwickshire
- ☐ **B)** Leicestershire
- ☐ **C)** Surrey
- ☐ **D)** Sussex

16. Why was one 2004 episode of children's television show *Peppa Pig* deemed 'unsuitable for broadcast' in Australia?

- ☐ **A)** Stoking lazy Australian stereotypes
- ☐ **B)** Spreading inaccurate information about marsupials
- ☐ **C)** Disrespecting Indigenous Australian traditions
- ☐ **D)** Reassuring about spiders

17. Which was the first British film to win best picture at the Academy Awards?

- ☐ **A)** *Tom Jones*
- ☐ **B)** *Hamlet*
- ☐ **C)** *Goodbye Mr Chips*
- ☐ **D)** *Oliver!*

18. Which country is consistently found to be Britain's favourite holiday destination?

- ☐ **A)** France
- ☐ **B)** Italy
- ☐ **C)** Spain
- ☐ **D)** The US

19. In the 1914 *Oxford Survey of the British Empire*, which was the first ailment discussed among 'problems of health and acclimatisation in the British dominions beyond the seas'?

☐ **A)** Tuberculosis

☐ **B)** Alcoholism

☐ **C)** Cholera

☐ **D)** Diphtheria

20. Which British singer inadvertently triggered a race controversy while performing on live television in America in April 1968?

☐ **A)** Petula Clark

☐ **B)** Cilla Black

☐ **C)** Marianne Faithfull

☐ **D)** Dusty Springfield

21. In the late 1980s, what did actor Michael Caine leave Britain for the United States in protest over?

☐ **A)** The tax rate

☐ **B)** Typecasting

☐ **C)** The Tory party

☐ **D)** The weather

22. In 2018, English writer and lyricist Tim Rice became history's fourteenth EGOT winner – meaning he has an Emmy, a Grammy, an Oscar and a Tony. Which of his works won an award first?

☐ **A)** *The Lion King*

☐ **B)** *Aladdin*

☐ **C)** *Evita*

☐ **D)** *Jesus Christ Superstar Live in Concert*

23. Only one of the below public figures was born in England. Who?

☐ **A)** Joanna Lumley

☐ **B)** Richard E. Grant

☐ **C)** Richard Curtis

☐ **D)** Eddie Redmayne

24. Which iconic British character or characters were given the keys to New York City?

☐ **A)** Paddington Bear

☐ **B)** The Teletubbies

☐ **C)** Peppa Pig

☐ **D)** Winnie-the-Pooh

25. Which of the below authors did NOT, at some point, spy for Britain?

☐ **A)** Ian Fleming

☐ **B)** Roald Dahl

☐ **C)** Graham Greene

☐ **D)** Anthony Horowitz

A. 24b

Answers

1. Weather

1.– A. The Beast from the East – The 'cold wave' wreaked havoc in February 2018, though the phrase is also used generally by the Met Office to describe cold and wintry conditions caused by easterly winds.

2.– A. Downpour – The reason that showers are so localized and unpredictable in the UK is because of the great variation in the ground-surface temperature, heating the air close to the ground at different rates. That's why showers can pop up anywhere. And do!

3.– B. 1814 – Sadly, we will never see another Frost Fair on the River Thames: climate change, the construction of the new London Bridge and dredging and embanking through the Victorian era have made it impossible.

4.– D. 6 hours – Its streak was broken by a rainbow in the Taiwanese capital of Taipei that lasted for eight hours and fifty-eight minutes.

5.– A. The name of a sea area was changed – The name Finisterre, used in the forecast to describe an area off north-west Spain since

1949, was renamed FitzRoy following complaints of confusion from Spain (which uses the term for a slightly different area).

6.– D. Watch and chain – 'Watch and chain' is (admittedly poorly used) cockney rhyming slang for 'brain'. You know the others, no?

7.– C. Michael Fish – Michael Fish served from 1974 to 2004 and was remembered before his final broadcast as 'the last of the true weathermen'. Of course, he is still remembered for the hurricane controversy, and 'the Michael Fish moment'.

8.– A. Fish fell from the sky – Fresh herring fell on the fields over the island of Islay, some still alive. In Mountain Ash, Glamorganshire, a sawyer named John Lewis described feeling 'something falling all over me . . . I was surprised to find they were little fish.'

9.– C. 1954 – Met Office forecast officer George Cowling pioneered 'in-vision' weather forecasting on the BBC on 11 January 1954, months before the first newsreader. He said the following day would be good for drying washing.

10.– B. Abigail – Storm Abigail was the first storm to be named jointly by the Met Office and Ireland's Met Éireann as part of its 'Name our Storms' project, with a name chosen from a selection sent in by the public.

11.– A. More rain (for forty days) – According to the old saying, rain on St Swithin's Day augurs rain for the next forty days, while no rain means the next forty days will be dry. There is absolutely no evidence in support of this.

12.– D. 8 – While the Centre Court has been protected by a retractable roof since 2009, the other courts are still at the mercy of the elements. According to analysis, the likelihood of it staying completely dry between the hours of 11 a.m. and 6 p.m. is only about one in four, or for rain to fall once every seven hours.

13.– D. 16 months – The exceptionally dry period began in May 1975 and was declared over only in September 1976, after water restrictions had been passed into law. For fifteen consecutive days from June, temperatures in Britain reached over 32 degrees Celsius.

14.– B. Held a day of fasting – With the storm considered to be an Act of God, the government declared 19 January 1704 a day of fasting, to acknowledge the 'crying sins of this nation' and 'the deepest and most solemn humiliation of our people'.

15.– A. 2017 – Ben Nevis was found to be without snow for the first time in eleven years in August 2017, due to less snowfall the previous winter.

16.– C. 'Scorchio!' – The 'Chanel 9 Neus' meteorologist Poula Fisch (played by Caroline Aherne) gave a forecast for a fictional Mediterranean country, where the temperature never fell below 45 degrees Celsius.

17.– D. Possible snow – Generally considered the dividing line between rain and snow, the lower the 528 line (5,280 metres above the surface of the Earth), the colder the air mass.

ANSWERS

18.– A. Scotland – Since 2011, Scotland has typically had the most rainfall in the UK. In 2011, it peaked at 1,862 millimetres, versus 712.8 millimetres in England.

19.– D. Blinter – That's a Scottish term for a gust of wind.

20.– A. Duckworth-Lewis-Stern – The method was devised by statisticians Frank Duckworth and Tony Lewis, and officially adopted by the ICC in 1999. Professor Steven Stern replaced them as 'custodian' of the method after their retirements and was included in the title in November 2014.

21.– B. Custard winds – Some etymologists believe the custard part probably originates from the word 'coastward'.

22.– C. A storm in May – 'Cow-quaker' refers to storms in May, after farmers let cows into their fields (a 'lambing storm' is a light spring snowfall).

23.– A. Durham – On 14 March 1947 the deepest ever recorded depth of snow lying in an inhabited location in the UK was measured at Forest-in-Teesdale in County Durham at 211 centimetres (83 inches).

24.– D. 'Trees uprooted; considerable structural damage; sea surface is largely white' – The scale was devised in 1805 by the Irish hydrographer Francis Beaufort to standardize weather observations, distinguishing one person's 'stiff breeze' from another's 'soft breeze'.

25.– A. Westminster Abbey – Westminster Abbey appears in the scene of the Bayeux Tapestry showing the funeral procession of Edward the Confessor, in which a man is attaching a weathervane to it.

2. Food and Drink

1.– C. Houses of Parliament – Frederick Gibson Garton, a grocer from Nottingham who developed the original recipe, registered the name H.P. Sauce in 1895 after hearing that a restaurant in the Houses of Parliament had begun serving it.

2.– D. Scones – In the 1700s, when tea parties became popular, the top tier was the only one that a warming dome would fit over. The middle tier was for sandwiches, and the bottom tier for sweets, pastries and desserts.

3.– A. Heinz – The H. J. Heinz Company was founded by the American entrepreneur Henry John Heinz in Pennsylvania in 1869.

4.– B. Pre-Gest – This referred to the tea's 'pre-digestive' qualities, with 'tips' later added to highlight that only the top two leaves and bud of each plant were used.

5.– A. A whole lemon – A Sussex pond pudding, or well pudding, is a traditional English pudding made of a suet pastry filled with butter, sugar and an entire baked lemon. Prue Leith calls it 'surely the epitome of Britishness'.

6.– C. £2.50 – Correct at time of writing, at least.

7.– B. Increased sales after a steady decline – The film precipitated a 3 per cent increase in sales of marmalade in the UK after four years of decline, according to analysis of supermarket data by research firm Kantar.

8.– A. Fish paste – Delicious! The creamy fish paste was replaced with sausage meat when Scotch eggs began to be commercially made and sold, as it was easier to package – and perhaps less offensive on trains.

9.– B. Squirrel casserole – The other three appeared in Cradock's recipe book *The Practical Cook*, published in 1949 when food rationing was still in force. It was a huge hit.

10.– B. Champagne – The combination was created in 1861, following the death of Albert, Prince Consort of Queen Victoria. So the story goes, a bar steward at Brook's Club said that even a glass of bubbly should be in mourning black.

11.– D. Browns Instantly, Seasons and Thickens in One – The first full-page advert for the product appeared in the *Daily Mail* on 4 February 1910. The slogan 'Ah! Bisto' appeared in the first large marketing campaign nine years later.

12.– E. All of the above – The Wombles, Basil Brush and Sooty appeared in television spots while Wallace and Gromit lent their faces to 'unique collectible moulds'. What better way to enjoy strawberry pudding.

13.– A. 4 billion – Sainsbury's supermarket alone sells around 436,800 sandwiches every thirty-six hours.

14.– D. Sultanas – The original recipe was invented by writer Constance Spry and Rosemary Hume, founder of the famous Le Cordon Bleu cookery school, and did not contain a single sultana.

15.– A. Joseph Fry – Joseph Fry mixed cocoa powder, sugar and cocoa butter into a paste that could be moulded into a solid chocolate bar in 1847 – gaining the attention of one John Cadbury, who followed suit with his own bar two years later.

16.– C. Easter eggs – Dubbed 'the Easter bunny' by police, Joby Pool stole almost 200,000 Cadbury Creme Eggs after breaking into a Telford industrial unit with a metal grinder.

17.– D. Prime Monster – Monster Munch crisps were originally launched in 1977 as Prime Monster, riffing on 'prime minister' as part of a wider campaign. It was changed to Monster Munch the following year.

18.– B. Fish heads – Traditionally, this Cornish pie is filled with whole pilchards, their heads poking through the pastry so that they may gaze upon the stars (as it were).

19.– D. Stovie – A cob is from the East Midlands, a bara is Welsh, and a stotty is eaten in Yorkshire. But a stovie is a Scottish meat, potato and onion stew.

20.– B. Soup – A simple South Indian broth called pepper water was adapted into a curried soup and quickly became a common dish among Britons living in India in the eighteenth century.

21.– A. Glasgow – Ali Ahmed Aslam was said to have invented the spice-chicken dish in 1964 at his restaurant, Shish Mahal, in Glasgow.

22.– B. Different meats – While the three dishes are very similar, a shepherd's pie is generally made with lamb, a cottage pie with beef, while a Cumberland can be either.

23.– C. 51 – Matt Ellis holds the record, according to *The Guinness Book of Records*, for the most pubs visited in twenty-four hours, visiting fifty-one pubs in Cambridgeshire in October 2021.

24.– A. Fizzy drink – The song was inspired by a pub in Leeds called the Fforde Grene; guitarist Boff Whalley said it was intended as a testament to 'the resilience of ordinary people'.

25.– B. Egg – The buck rarebit, otherwise known as a golden buck, is made by adding an egg to a Welsh rarebit.

3. History

1.– D. The government – The phrase was one of three key propaganda messages coined by the shadowy Ministry of Information ahead of the Second World War. The others were 'Your courage, your cheerfulness, your resolution – will bring us victory' and 'Freedom is in peril; defend it with all your might.'

2.– A. Statistician – 'The lady with the lamp' was also a pioneer of data visualization, developing graphics and charts to publicize the need for sanitary reform.

3.– C. The International Web – The Web was not Berners-Lee's first information design system. In 1980 he wrote ENQUIRE, named after a Victorian era how-to book called *Enquire Within upon Everything*, owned by Berners-Lee's parents while he was growing up.

4.– B. The Great Fire of London – The Great Fire of London began on 2 September in Thomas Farriner's bakery on Pudding Lane. In four days, one third of London's buildings were destroyed, 86 per cent of the City was burnt to the ground and 130,000 people were made homeless. Remarkably, only six lives were lost.

5.– A. The English Civil War – In this seventeenth-century conflict, more than 185,000 died, which amounted to 10 per cent of all the adult males in England.

6.– D. Lindisfarne – The bloody Viking attack on the church of St Cuthbert, on the Holy Island in present-day Northumberland, sent a shockwave through Europe.

7.– A. James I – Though Guy Fawkes persists today as a symbol of left-wing protests and countercultural upheaval, this misrepresents his name: his aim was not to overthrow the government but to install a new king.

8.– C. First patient – Sylvia Beckingham, then thirteen, was admitted to hospital in Manchester with liver problems on 5 July 1948 as the first patient of the NHS.

9.– A. The residents of Aberfan – The Welsh Secretary of State George Thomas ordered £150,000 for the remaining coal tips' removal to come from donations made to the village, a decision that was heavily criticized.

10.– B. Developing the steam engine – In 1778, James Watt and Matthew Boulton invented a steam engine that could efficiently power factory machinery.

11.– B. The Whitechapel Bell Foundry – The Whitechapel Bell Foundry cast bells for 500 years from the reign of Queen Elizabeth I and there is still a bell foundry situated in a heritage-listed building in the East End of London.

12.– A. Sea Lion – Operation Sea Lion was the code name for Nazi Germany's planned invasion of Britain. It was supposed to take place in September 1940 and, had it been successful, would have completed Adolf Hitler's domination of western Europe.

13.– D. Manchester – Manchester's population grew from 90,000 at the 1801 census to 543,900 by 1901. At that time, London already had a population of 6 million.

14.– D. National Covenant – The document was signed at Greyfriars Kirk in Edinburgh, a location best known for the legend of a loyal dog called Bobby.

ANSWERS

15.– A. Land of the Angles – The Angles of Denmark were one of two main tribes to settle in Great Britain during the Early Middle Ages. The second tribe, the Saxons, arrived from Germany. Most indigenous English people can trace their ancestry back to the Anglo-Saxons.

16.– C. French – From 1066 to 1362, French was an official language due to the invasion of William the Conquerer.

17.– C. Astrophysicist Jocelyn Bell-Burnell – The £50 note displaying astrophysicist Dame Jocelyn Bell-Burnell was shortlisted for the World Banknote of the Year Awards in 2023.

18.– A. Easter Monday – The Rising began on Easter Monday, 24 April 1916, and lasted for just six days. At the ceasefire on Saturday 29 April, the 2,500-odd rebels were faced by around 20,000 British troops.

19.– D. The first women to matriculate at a British university – Led by Sophia Jex-Blake, the Edinburgh Seven became the first women to enrol to study at a British university, to study medicine.

20.– A. Their 'second-best bed' – Historians dispute whether Shakespeare's bequest of their 'second-best bed' to his wife, Anne, was a deliberate snub; either way, it is likely to have been their marital bed, with the 'best bed' reserved for guests.

21.– C. 479 – The Domesday Book focused on landowners and male workers, who at the time were overwhelmingly men.

22.– D. All three – Bubonic plague affects the lymphatic system, pneumonic plague the lungs, and septicaemic plague the blood. It is thought likely that all three played some role in the pandemic.

23.– A. Her young son – Queen Margaret's seven-year-old son decreed that the Yorkists should 'have their heads taken off', and she complied.

24.– B. Marengo – According to legend, the grey Arab horse was captured during the Egyptian campaign and was ridden by Napoleon through all his famous campaigns. Marengo's skeleton is kept at the National Army Museum in London.

25.– C. 45 minutes – This 1896 stand-off between the British Royal Navy and the Sultanate of Zanzibar may have lasted as little as thirty-eight minutes, but it generated a surprisingly high number of casualties.

4. Football

1.– D. Scotland – The 1872 match is officially recognized by FIFA as the sport's first international. It was watched by 4,000 spectators and ended in a 0–0 draw.

2.– A. Celtic – The 1966–7 season of the European Cup was won by Celtic for the first time in the final against Internazionale, who eliminated defending champions Real Madrid in the quarter-finals, making Celtic the first British team in history to win the trophy.

3.– B. Paul Gascoigne – After his former manager Bobby Robson was quoted as calling Gazza 'daft as a brush' in the press, Gazza went to training with a brush sticking out of the top of his sock.

4.– A. Sweden – Hosts England won their first UEFA Women's Championship title by beating Germany 2–1 after extra time in the final, held at Wembley Stadium in London.

5.– C. Sir Bobby Charlton – Designed by Scottish architect Archibald Leitch and inaugurated in 1910, with its nearly 75,000 seats it is the largest club stadium in the United Kingdom.

6.– C. Eric Cantona – A total of thirty-nine perfect hat-tricks have been scored in the Premier League since 1992.

7.– D. To boost archery – Edward's subsequent Archery Law, passed two years later, required all Englishmen to practise with a bow on Sundays and made any sport that interfered with this illegal.

8.– A. No more than six players to a side – There is in fact no limit on the number of players, and very few rules. Shrovetide ball games have been played in England since at least the twelfth century, from the reign of Henry II (1154–89).

9.– D. A UEFA Cup game between Liverpool and Danish side Brondby – The match resulted in a tie.

10.– C. Green and gold – Fans still display the colours of the club's founding fathers, Newton Heath, as a sign of rebellion against the current ownership.

11.– B. Martin Peters – The goal gave rise to one of the most famous calls in English football history, when BBC commentator Kenneth Wolstenholme declared, 'They think it's all over.'

12.– D. Antonio Conte – Conte, who had been struggling with baldness, arrived at Stamford Bridge with a full head of hair amid rumours of transplant surgery.

13.– B. Resisting quarantine of his pet dog.

14.– A. Fara Williams – Williams played at the 2005, 2009, 2013 and 2017 European Championships, as well as the World Cups in 2007, 2011 and 2015, before announcing her retirement in 2021.

15.– B. Clarence Seedorf – Seedorf won with Ajax, Real Madrid and AC Milan.

16.– B. Nigel Clough – To date he's managed Burton Albion, Derby County, Sheffield United and Mansfield Town.

17.– D. The Bluebirds – The name by which Cardiff City is known.

18.– C. Total Network Solutions – The 1997 name change was the first instance in the United Kingdom of a football club renaming itself after its sponsor.

19.– A. Sheffield United – Though Manchester United was founded earlier, in 1878 as Newton Heath LYR FC, it was renamed in 1902.

20.– B. Ryan Giggs – Ryan Giggs holds the record for the most assists in Premier League history, with 162 to his name.

21.– A. Wanderers FC – The 1872 FA Cup final between Wanderers and Royal Engineers was held on 16 March 1872 at Kennington Oval in London. The final score was 1–0.

22.– D. Cardiff City – Unfortunately, they were relegated in 2014.

23.– C. Aston Villa – Six keepers have scored in Premier League games: Schmeichel in 2001, Brad Friedel in 2004, Paul Robinson in 2007, Tim Howard in 2012, Asmir Begović in 2013 and Alisson Becker in 2021.

24.– D. Andrew Watson – Watson earned the first of his three caps for Scotland on 12 March 1881, captaining the side to a 6–1 win away to England at the Oval in London.

25.– A. Kris Boyd – He scored 167 for Kilmarnock and Rangers.

5. Sport

1.– C. 11 hours – The longest tennis match lasted for eleven hours and five minutes and was played over three days between John Isner and Nicolas Mahut in 2010.

2.– A. Harry Vardon – Harry Vardon won six British Open Titles, in 1896, 1898, 1899, 1903, 1911 and 1914.

3.– A. His younger brother – After leading the nearly two-hour race, Jonny Brownlee collapsed from heat exhaustion; his older brother Alistair half carried him for the remaining 500 metres, ceding first place to Henri Schoeman from South Africa.

4.– D. Lewis Hamilton – Lewis Hamilton has won the most titles of any driver representing the UK, level with Michael Schumacher for most titles. Hamilton is still active in the sport.

5.– C. Snowboarding – Brookes started snowboarding when she was just eighteen months old.

6.– B. Crochet – After being spotted knitting at the Tokyo Games, Daley put out his own book of knitting and crochet patterns and sells kits under the brand name Made With Love.

7.– D. Lord's – The Nursery End is the north-east end of the pitch, facing the Pavilion End, where the main members' pavilion is located.

8.– A. Jack Hobbs – Known as 'The Master', Hobbs is widely regarded as one of the greatest batsmen in the history of cricket, with 61,237 runs and 197 centuries.

9.– B. England v Scotland – Awarded since 1879, the Calcutta Cup is made from melted down Indian rupees donated by the Calcutta Club.

10.– A. New Zealand – England and New Zealand have been playing each other in test rugby since 1905, but England has only won eight games to the All Blacks' thirty-three.

11.– B. Cricket and rugby union – Alan represented his country against Scotland at Murrayfield, while Chris played for England against the West Indies in the Caribbean.

12.– C. Codebreaker Alan Turing – Though a talented long-distance runner, Turing came in fifth place at a qualifying marathon for the 1948 Olympics. Actor Jason Statham also came up short in qualifying for diving at the 1992 games.

13.– B. Cycling – Kenny won his seventh gold in the men's keirin at Tokyo 2020, putting him one ahead of his fellow track-cycling specialist Sir Chris Hoy.

14.– A. Glasgow – Scotland has hosted the Commonwealth Games three times, Edinburgh in 1970 and 1986 and Glasgow in 2014.

15.– D. Change from a tenner – Davis won £6 and ten shillings, raised from ticket sales. The winner of the 2023 event received £500,000.

16.– A. 6 weeks – Australian John Landy beat Bannister's record by more than a second. Now close to 1,500 people have run a mile in under four minutes.

17.– C. Alun Wyn Jones – With 170 caps in total, Wales's Wyn Jones beats the All Blacks' Richie McCaw and Sam Whitelock for the most caps in rugby history.

18.– C. 16 – Taylor has won more than 210 professional tournaments, including 85 major titles.

19.– A. Furocity – Fury launched Furocity in February 2022, branding industry leaders Red Bull and Monster 'dossers' and 'chickens'.

20.– B. Juan Martin del Potro – Andy Murray became the first male player to win two Olympic tennis golds after beating Juan Martin del Potro 7–5, 4–6, 6–2, 7–5 in Rio.

21.– D. A fence jumped in the Grand National

22.– A. A sailor faked his location – Donald Crowhurst reported false locations in an attempt to fake having completed the circumnavigation, then disappeared in an apparent suicide.

23.– D. Drooler – Please don't ask us to explain them.

24.– B. Croquet – One of the first sports that allowed men and women to play on equal terms, croquet was the foundation sport of Wimbledon until the early 1920s.

25.– A. Virginia Wade – Wade was ranked in the world's top ten for thirteen consecutive years, winning three singles titles and four doubles titles in Grand Slam tournaments.

6. Music

1.– A. Sting – The 71-year-old musician joins the likes of Paul Mc-Cartney, Peter Gabriel, Kate Bush, Joan Armatrading, Elton John and Annie Lennox as an Ivors fellow.

2.– C. Lonnie Donegan – Donegan pioneered the 'skiffle' genre, blending blues, jazz and American folk. 'He was the man,' said Paul McCartney.

3.– D. Cliff Richard – His latest album, *Music . . . the Air that I Breathe*, reached number three in November 2020.

4.– A. Evelyn Dove – Evelyn Dove, a cabaret singer popular from the 1920s, was a contemporary of Josephine Baker and was broadcast singing on BBC Radio only three years after it was launched.

5.– B. Hubert Parry – Parry set 'Jerusalem' to music, intending to lift the nation's spirits during the First World War, but it was soon adopted by the women's suffrage movement.

6.– B. John Barry – John Barry composed the scores for eleven of the James Bond films between 1963 and 1987, as well as arranging and performing the theme for 1962's *Dr No*.

7.– C. Cow – Although a cow does appear on the cover of the 1970 Pink Floyd album *Atom Heart Mother*.

8.– A. 'Nimrod' by Edward Elgar – Elgar appears on the Bank of England's £20 note.

ANSWERS

9.– D. Delia Derbyshire – Derbyshire worked at the BBC's fledgling Radiophonic Workshop in the 1960s.

10.– A. 'Relax' by Frankie Goes to Hollywood – The Liverpool group's overt sexual innuendo was highly controversial in the UK, not least because it featured two gay men.

11.– A. George Bridgetower – In January 1789, when Bridgetower was only ten years old, he was written of as 'the greatest phenomenon ever heard'.

12.– D. Shirley Temple – Child actress Shirley Temple appears barely visible behind the wax models of John and Ringo; in the front row; and as a cloth doll.

13.– B. Their friends worked at a pet shop – 'We thought it sounded like an English rap group,' said Neil Tennant.

14.– B. Dave – Dave, who won Album of the Year with *Psychodrama*, also called for support for the Windrush generation and castigated the media over their coverage of Meghan Markle in a freestyle performance of 'Black'.

15.– C. Coldplay – Chris Martin said the name was chosen 'out of absolute necessity' an hour before their first gig. By the second, their name was The Coldplay.

16.– D. The time he spent making it – Stormzy's first mixtape was put together in one week, or 168 hours.

17.– A. The Laughing Gnome – Bowie duetted with The Laughing Gnome in his early hit of the same name, having earlier appeared on the BBC at the age of seventeen to defend his long locks.

18.– B. Sheeran's albums in order, are +, ×, ÷, *No. 6 Collaborations Project*, = and –. It is very annoying.

19.– C. Nicole Scherzinger – The Pussycat Dolls ringleader earned her spot performing at King Charles III's coronation for this alone.

20.– D. The Blues Boys – This was the former name of The Rolling Stones.

21.– A. Rapper Nas – In the song, Winehouse laments being forced to miss a Nas concert, possibly his show at the Brixton Academy in March 2005. Nas featured Winehouse on his song 'Cherry Wine'.

22.– C. 2000 – The Spice Girls announced their hiatus in December 2000. 'Viva Forever'.

23.– C. The Just Brothers' 'Sliced Tomatoes' – Fatboy Slim's 'The Rockafeller Skank' sampled the guitar riff alongside a wealth of other samples.

24.– D. Butter – Lydon defended himself against criticisms of selling out with his spot for Country Life butter, saying he was 'very proud' to promote a British product and that part of his multimillion-pound fee went towards touring with PiL.

25.– A. P. J. Harvey – Harvey won in 2001 with *Stories from the City, Stories from the Sea* and again in 2011 with *Let England Shake*.

7. Art and Fashion

1.– D. Alexander McQueen – The Princess of Wales's dress was designed by Sarah Burton, the creative director of the luxury fashion house Alexander McQueen. It now has its own Wikipedia page.

2.– D. Hedgehog – The humble hedgehog has so far escaped Damien Hirst's attentions. One analysis estimated that nearly 1 million animals had been put to use in his art.

3.– A. A stab-proof vest bearing the Union Jack – Stormzy's stab vest was designed by Banksy and was worn to draw attention to rising rates of knife crime in London.

4.– A. Stanley Donwood – Donwood has created all the artwork for Radiohead since 1994, as well as for singer Thom Yorke's other projects.

5.– C. *Zoolander* – Moss does, however, appear in *Zoolander 2*.

6.– B. A haircut – Legendary hairdresser Vidal Sassoon was inspired by the 1920 Bauhaus school for his five-point bob cut, describing it as a feat of 'pure geometry'.

7.– C. Dismaland – Set up in a disused lido in Weston-super-Mare, Dismaland was billed as 'a theme park unsuitable for children'.

ANSWERS

8.– C. Edward Enninful – Enninful was the first man and the first Black person to be made editor-in-chief of British *Vogue*. In 2023 it was announced that he would be moving to a new global role.

9.– A. No underwear – Vivienne Westwood claimed to never wear underwear with dresses or skirts, and her twirl in the Buckingham Palace courtyard left photographers in no doubt.

10.– B. The French army's underwear – Selfridges lost the contract to supply the British army uniforms to Harrods.

11.– D. Tracey Emin – Emin was nominated for the 1999 Turner Prize with her famously intimate installation *My Bed*, but did not win.

12.– A. Belleek – Ireland's oldest pottery, Belleek china fetches high prices at auction.

13.– B. Barbara Hepworth – Her home and studio in St Ives, Cornwall, is now a museum.

14.– C. It was covered with real butterfly wings – Sotheby's sold Damien Hirst's *Butterfly Bike* at auction for $500,000.

15.– D. Sugar cubes – Sugar merchant Tate donated his contemporary art collection and £80,000 to the government for the Tate Galleries and introduced sugar cubes to the UK.

16.– A. Thomas Gainsborough – *The Blue Boy* was once the most famous painting in the world.

17.– D. The 2001 foot-and-mouth crisis – At the time of writing, no musical has been made of the 2001 foot-and-mouth crisis – not to give anyone any ideas.

18.– A. Apollo Victoria – The Apollo Victoria can hold an audience of nearly 2,400 people, compared to the Fortune Theatre, which has a capacity of just 432 people.

19.– B. Tom Hiddleston – The three-week production was a fund-raiser for the Royal Academy of Dramatic Art.

20.– B. J. M. W. Turner – Turner, described as 'arguably the single most influential British artist of all time', features on the £20 banknote.

21.– C. Clore Studio – The Clore Studio is at Tate Britain, a mistake you only make once. Tate Modern's Boiler House was renamed the Natalie Bell Building in 2018.

22.– C. Bridget Riley – Riley's work was central to the Op Art move-ment and she was successful on both sides of the Atlantic from the mid-1960s.

23.– D. Sonia Boyce – Boyce's work entered Tate Modern's per-manent collection in 1987 but she was elected as a Royal Academician only in 2016.

24.– A. Topshop – Topshop became the first ever high-street fash-ion brand to show at London Fashion Week in 2005, and it did so until 2018.

25.– C. Gilbert and George – Gilbert and George's show *Jack Freak Pictures* made heavy use of the Union flag, with the artists picturing themselves in Union flag bondage masks and alongside a crucified Christ.

8. Film

1.– C. Marwood – His name is never stated in the film, but appears on an envelope in one scene.

2.– D. *The Third Man* – *The Third Man* is based on the novel by Graham Greene (though du Maurier is alleged to have had an affair with the director, Carol Reed).

3.– A. Bernard – Famously, every Curtis film includes a grumpy character named Bernard for a specific reason: Tory MP Bernard Jenkin stole Curtis's girlfriend at university.

4.– B. The aqualung briefcase – A knife shoe saves the day in *From Russia with Love*, explosive toothpaste in *Licence to Kill*; and, yes, an attack sofa preposterously features in *The Living Daylights*.

5.– D. *Churchill* – Greenwood also has an ongoing collaboration with Paul Thomas Anderson, scoring *Inherent Vice*, *There Will be Blood* and *Phantom Thread*.

6.– A. *Porno* – The book catches up with the characters of *Trainspotting* ten years later.

7.– B. 27 – James Bond has been portrayed on screen in a total of twenty-seven productions, but two are unlicensed and as such not recognized as part of the canon.

8.– A. Helen Mirren – Unlike, apparently, every single one of her peers, Helen Mirren did not receive an owl inviting her to Hogwarts. She did, however, host a televised Harry Potter quiz.

9.– B. The Black Knight – The Black Knight is a memorable character in *Monty Python and the Holy Grail*.

10.– B. 8 minutes – Dench is in good company: Anthony Hopkins, Ingrid Bergman, Penelope Cruz, Kim Basinger, David Niven and Anne Hathaway all won Oscars for roles with less than twenty minutes' screentime.

11.– D. Sheffield – In 2003, Disney released its television reboot of *The Full Monty*, featuring members of the original cast and also shot in Sheffield.

12.– A. She was pregnant – Julie Andrews was pregnant when she was offered the part of Mary Poppins, and turned it down, but Disney said they would wait for her to start filming.

13.– C. *Mary Poppins* – Julie Andrews' first ever film, *Mary Poppins*, was Disney's highest-grossing film to date and received thirteen Academy Award nominations including Best Picture.

14.– A. *Lock, Stock and Two Smoking Barrels* – *Lock, Stock and Two Smoking Barrels* was dedicated to Lenny McLean, who played

Barry the Baptist and died of cancer one month before the film opened in England.

15.– B. *Rye Lane* – The romcom, set in Peckham, features a cameo from Colin Firth.

16.– A. *Moonraker* – Bassey sang the theme to this 1979 Bond film, with Roger Moore as 007.

17.– C. *Bird* – The film was inspired by Barry Hines' book *A Kestrel for a Knave.*

18.– D. Charles Darwin – Cumberbatch did appear in Jon Amiel's film about Charles Darwin, *Creation*, but played the botanist Joseph Hooker.

19.– B. *That Sinking Feeling* – The 1979 comedy *That Sinking Feeling* is set in Bill Forsyth's home city of Glasgow and stars members of the city's Youth Theatre. Its tagline was 'eight teenagers . . . ninety sinks . . . and the crime of the century!'

20.– A. *The Wicker Man* – The 1973 original *Wicker Man*, declared 'the *Citizen Kane* of horror', was remade with Nicolas Cage in the starring role.

21.– D. Fear of dogs – Hitchcock loved dogs but talked to a journalist of his ovophobia in 1963: 'I'm frightened of eggs. Worse than frightened – they revolt me.' Chicken eggs were said to be a particular trigger.

22.– B. Patrick Dempsey – Patrick Dempsey, or McDreamy from *Grey's Anatomy*, joined *Bridget Jones's Baby* as a too-good-to-be-true tech entrepreneur.

23.– D. Three Flavours Cornetto – A riff on the French Three Colours trilogy by Krzysztof Kieślowski, Wright's Three Flavours Cornetto trilogy encompasses *Shaun of the Dead* (Strawberry), *Hot Fuzz* (Classico) and *The World's End* (Mint).

24.– C. The 1950s – As well as Best British Film at the BAFTAs, *Brooklyn* was also nominated for three Academy Awards, including Best Actress for Saoirse Ronan.

25.– D. John Boyega – Boyega publicly called out director Abrams and Disney for sidelining his character, Finn, a stormtrooper turned resistance fighter.

9. TV

1.– C. Jon Pertwee

2.– A. Crinkley Bottom

3.– C. *Good Morning Britain*

4.– D. Channel 4

5.– A. *Brass Eye*

6.– A. Northern Ireland – While many of *GoT*'s recurring sets (like the Iron Throne room) are filmed at Paint Hall studios in Belfast, the show was largely shot on location in Northern Ireland and in Iceland, Croatia and Spain.

7.– D. 'Here's one I made earlier.'

8.– C. Mr Cauliflower – Mr White was also considered as a moniker for Mr Bean.

9.– B. *Pingu* – The 'Little Accidents' episode of *Pingu* was removed from circulation on the strength of its 'heavy focus on uncensored urination and toilet humour'.

10.– A. *Quiz* – Matthew Macfadyen played Charles Ingram, the British army major who was accused of cheating on *Who Wants to be a Millionaire* in September 2001.

11.– D. Sarah Snook – Sarah Snook is Australian, while Brian Cox is Scottish, Matthew Macfadyen is – of course – English, and Annabelle Dexter-Jones is British-American.

12.– B. The popularity of Coldplay – Super Hans dismisses Jeremy's faith in humankind: 'People like Coldplay and voted for the Nazis. You can't trust people.'

13.– A. Craig Phillips

14.– C. Will Poulter

ANSWERS

15.– B. *'Allo 'Allo*

16.– D. Matt Lucas – Nothing stays the same in the *Bake-Off* Tent: just as Matt Lucas replaced Sandi Toksvig, now Alison Hammond is replacing Matt Lucas.

17.– D. Lulu

18.– D. 2006

19.– B. Agnes

20.– B. The perfect body

21.– D. Helen Mirren – She played the queen in the film *The Queen*.

22.– C. *What Can I Bring?*

23.– A. Michael Parkinson pretended to be possessed by a demon live on air

24.– C. The Garrison Tavern

25.– A. E20

10. Politics

1.– A. Robert Walpole – Robert Walpole led the government of the Kingdom of Great Britain for over twenty years from 1721, and is generally taken to be the first prime minister – though, strictly speaking, the first prime minister of the United Kingdom of Great Britain and Ireland was William Pitt the Younger.

2.– C. 'Seven Nation Army' by The White Stripes – When Corbyn appeared on stage just before the Libertines at the Wirral Live rock festival in May 2017, somebody – nobody quite knows who – started the chant and the crowd took it up immediately.

3.– A. William Pitt the Younger

4.– A. Clement Attlee

5.– D. 1971 – The unionist, loyalist and national conservative political party in Northern Ireland was co-founded in 1971 during the Troubles by Ian Paisley, who led the party for the next thirty-seven years.

6.– B. 6 – The broadcast ban was enacted in October 1988 and lifted six years later, in September 1994 by prime minister John Major, shortly after the first Provisional IRA ceasefire.

7.– A. Labour

8.– C. Learie Constantine – Constantine became the first Black member of the House of Lords on 26 March 1969, and is also one of the best all-round cricketers the world has ever seen.

9.– B. Spencer Perceval – Perceval was shot dead in the lobby of the House of Commons in May 1812 by John Bellingham, an aggrieved merchant. Bellingham was put to death and Perceval's ministry was largely forgotten.

10.– A. Mr Whippy ice cream

11.– C. 2003

12.– D. 'Things Can Only Get Better' by D:Ream – The title claims that things 'cannot get worse'.

13.– A. Labour – The 2021 general election was the sixth since the Senedd was established (as the National Assembly for Wales) in 1999, and had the highest turnout ever.

14.– C. English Literature

15.– A. St Crispin's Day – Of course, this is the anniversary of the Battle of Agincourt, fought between English and French armies on 25 October 1415. Incidentally, St Crispin was the patron saint of cobblers.

16.– C. 50 days – Famously, a lettuce was shown to have a longer shelf life.

17.– B. Dana Scallon – Performing as Dana, Scallon won the 1970 Eurovision Song Contest with 'All Kinds of Everything', which became a worldwide million-seller and launched her music career. She entered politics in 1997.

18.– C. Ed Balls Day – In 2011, Ed Balls, then a Labour MP, had been attempting to search for his name on Twitter but entered it into the wrong field. His 2011 tweet reading only 'ed balls' remains live and is regularly recirculated.

19.– A. She ran through fields of wheat – Running through the fields of wheat, Theresa May explained, caused the local farmers displeasure. She was a 'bookish child', she concluded.

20.– D. Harriet Harman – Harman stepped down after nearly forty years in Parliament, having fought ten elections, served under seven prime ministers and eight Labour leaders.

21.– B. 249 – Since 2019, Lord Buckethead has been a candidate with the Official Monster Raving Loony Party.

22.– A. He was testing his eyesight

23.– C. 'Who governs Britain?' – Perhaps unsurprisingly, voters gravitated more towards Labour's optimistic message of 'Let us work together'. Labour captured 301 seats against the Conservatives' 297, setting the scene for another election in October.

24.– D. Labour candidate Stephen Twigg defeated Conservative cabinet minister Michael Portillo – The surprise announcement of Twigg's win, just after 3 a.m., was the first suggestion that the Tories might be out for the first time in eighteen years.

25.– A. Sinn Féin – Sinn Féin won twenty-seven seats, compared to the DUP's twenty-five.

11. Books

1.– B. How many seagulls are needed to lift James's giant peach? – The students concluded: 2,425,907 seagulls.

2.– B. 'Aero: Irrestibubble' – He also came up with 'Naughty but nice' for the UK Milk Board's cream cakes; for the *Mirror* newspaper: 'Look into the *Mirror* tomorrow - you'll like what you see'; and 'That'll do nicely' for American Express credit cards.

3.– A. Andrew Motion – Motion was Poet Laureate from May 1999 to May 2009, taking over from Ted Hughes.

4.– D. Teachers

5.– A. *Bleak House* – *Bleak House* is notably Dickens's only novel to feature a female narrator, the heroine Esther Summerson.

6.– D. She went missing for 11 days

7.– A. #Merky Books

8.– C. Timmy

9.– B. Todd's syndrome, which affects perception of size

10.– D. His own wife was secretly mentally ill, like Bertha Rochester

ANSWERS

11.– A. Martin

12.– C. Bathilda Bagshot

13.– C. Staples

14.– A. *Rebecca*

15.– B. Ian Fleming

16.– B. Oxfordshire

17.– D. Pop

18.– A. Mary Shelley

19.– D. *Girl, Woman, Other*

20.– B. 'One may as well begin with Jerome's emails to his father.'

21.– A. *Pride and Prejudice*

22.– D. Salman Rushdie – Margaret Atwood is the fourth double winner.

23.– A. *The Remains of the Day* by Kazuo Ishiguro

24.– C. *Shuggie Bain* by Douglas Stuart

25.– A. Lord Cochrane

12. Landscapes and Landmarks

1.– A. 13

2.– C. 75 miles

3.– D. Brixton – Brixton was the site of the nearest labour exchange.

4.– A. The Guinness Storehouse – The seven-storey tourist hotspot was erected in 1904, making it the first skyscraper in the British Isles.

5.– C. Great-grandfather and great-grandson – The archer is said to have died up to eighty years before his 'companion'.

6.– A. Creswell Crags – Directors of Creswell Heritage Trust had mistaken the apotropaic marks (symbols to ward off evil or misfortune) for 'Victorian graffiti'.

7.– B. Highclere Castle, Hampshire – Today, the 'real' Downton Abbey house is home to George Herbert and his wife, Fiona, the 8th Earl and Countess of Carnarvon.

8.– D. Seven and a half times the size of New York's Central Park – The Stonehenge part of the World Heritage Site covers 2,600 hectares (6,500 acres). For comparison, the Glastonbury festival site is around 1,100 hectares or 500 football pitches.

9.– A. Schiehallion – The Schiehallion experiment was an attempt to measure the mass of the Earth using a pendulum and a mountain. The mass of the mountain was approximated and the deflection of a pendulum due to the gravitational force of the mountain was measured.

10.- B. River Severn – At 220 miles long, the Severn rises near the River Wye on the north-eastern slopes of Plynlimon, Wales, then follows a semicircular course basically southward to the Bristol Channel and the Atlantic Ocean.

11.- B. Brokenwind – Brokenwind exists – but it's a little hamlet in Aberdeenshire, Scotland, not England.

12.- C. Harrods

13.- A. Nannie the witch

14.- D. Big Ben – Big Ben is the name given to the bell that chimes, not the famous clock face or the clock tower.

15.- D. Annual cheese-rolling competition

16.- A. Nearly 35,000

17.- B. A Newcastle United shirt

18.- C. Loch Lomond

19.- D. Taff – In the 1840s, Isambard Kingdom Brunel diverted the Taff to the west to create a larger and safer site for Cardiff

Central railway station. The station was opened by South Wales Railway in 1850.

20.– A. Queen of the Curve – Zaha Hadid's fluid, organic designs looked like they were in motion, earning her the name Queen of the Curve. The architect Elia Zenghelis, Hadid's teacher, called her 'the inventor of 89 degrees'.

21.– D. The Microwave

22.– D. Birmingham – Though it is named after the astronomer John Birmingham, not the city.

23.– B. A swan

24.– D. London Bridge – Pink Floyd's *The Animals* album shows Battersea Power Station; The Clash were pictured at Camden Market on their eponymous album; Wings posed on Tower Bridge for their sixth album *London Town* ... But what the Black-Eyed Peas' Fergie thinks is London Bridge is in fact Tower Bridge.

25.– A. *Empire Windrush* – MV *Monte Rosa* was built in Germany as a cruise ship, taking German travellers to Europe and South America on Nazi-approved holidays; its name was changed after it was captured by the British as a prize of war in 1945.

13. The Monarchy

1.– D. Operation London Bridge

ANSWERS

2.– A. Drina – Her official name was Alexandrina, after her godfather Tsar Alexander I of Russia. Victoria was her middle name.

3.– B. Elizabeth Arden Eight-hour Cream – Don't ask where he applied it, but it seemed to do the job.

4–D. £86 million a year – This annual sovereign grant payment from the Treasury also pays for other costs of the working royals, such as property maintenance and travel, but if Charles finds he's coming up short, there are means of increasing it.

5.– C. No tea to be taken after 7 p.m.

6.– B. King George II – In 1727.

7.– D. All of the above

8.– C. The nine-day queen – She had the shortest reign in British history.

9.– A. Frog – A species of tree frog, discovered in 2008 in Ecuador, was named after then Prince Charles to honour his commitment to rainforest conservation: it is the *Hyloscirtus princecherlesi*, or Prince Charles Magnificent Tree Frog.

10.– C. An hour alone – Growing up under the Kensington System, Victoria had been constantly accompanied by her mother, who even slept in her room. Her second request as queen was for a bedroom of her own.

11.– D. All of the above

12.– D. A miniature self-portrait by Charlie Chaplin.

13.– A. Weighing themselves on arrival and just before departure –
This confronting festive pastime of weighing guests pre- and
post-Christmas is supposed to give proof of your indulgence
and dates back to King Edward VII.

14.– B. A novelty Christmas sweater from William

15.– A. Edward the Caresser – Also known as 'The playboy prince',
Edward's purported lovers include the famous French actress
Sarah Bernhardt and Jennie Churchill, mother of Winston.

16.– C. Prince Charles and Lady Diana Spencer – Their 1981 nuptials
were watched by 750 million people in 74 countries, making
it the largest outside broadcast in British history. It had an
audience in Britain of 39 million. Princess Margaret's royal
wedding was the first to be televised and reached around
300 million viewers worldwide.

17.– B. Princess Anne – Princess Anne was made a 'Prime Warden' of
the guild of sellers of fish and seafood in 2017, having previously served in the guilds of 'carmen', 'woolmen' and farmers.

18.– A. The Tig

19.– D. A ceremonial 'hostage-taking' of an MP – While the monarch
is in Westminster, an MP is held 'hostage' in Buckingham

Palace so as to ensure the monarch's safe return, a tradition stemming from the time of King Charles I, who was convicted of treason and beheaded on 30 January 1649.

20.– B. Prince George of Cambridge

21.– A. 6 days old

22.– D. King George V – He also had a tattoo of a tiger; both were tattooed on him during a visit to Japan.

23.– C. Grouse – In other words, groussaka!

24.– B. Archewell – The Duke and Duchess of Sussex's organization Archewell claims to 'unleash the power of compassion to drive systemic cultural change'.

25.– C. By a modified Land Rover – The coffin of the late Duke of Edinburgh, who died on 9 April 2021 at the age of ninety-nine, was transported in a Land Rover Defender TD5 130 chassis cab vehicle that he had spent sixteen years modifying to be his hearse.

14. British Exceptionalism

1.– A. 531 million – On the eve of the Second World War.

2.– B. A quarter

3.– D. The atomic bomb

4.– A. 33 per cent – The average in Europe is closer to 60 per cent.

5.– A. The Himalayas

6.– D. India – India was excluded from the Balfour Declaration because of an active independence movement: its position within the empire was not settled, was the ominous word from the Commonwealth.

7.– D. Facial hair – Unfashionable in Britain but popular as a symbol of manliness in India, moustaches were made compulsory among the British Punjabi so they did not appear emasculated.

8.– A. Thomas Arne – Arne also composed the song 'A-Hunting We Will Go', a popular folk song and nursery rhyme.

9.– C. James Cook – In January 1773.

10.– B. Oceanography – In particular, the *Challenger's* expedition debunked the theory, popular at the time, that the ocean floor was covered with primordial ooze.

11.– A. Sea shanties

12.– D. Belgium – Decrees of 1946 and 1947 set legal time as one hour ahead of GMT.

13.– B. Bags of their own blood – In countries where a reliable blood supply is questionable, senior royals may be accompanied

ANSWERS

by the royal physician and their own personal supply of blood in case of an emergency transfusion.

14.– C. Partition in British India

15.– C. 'Pukka'

16.– A. South Africa – The Cullinan I diamond, presented to King Edward VII in 1907, is also known as the Great Star of Africa.

17.– D. Maintain fireplaces and build and tend fires

18.– B. Gabon and Togo – Both were formerly French territories.

19.– C. A life pension – At ten years old, Duleep Singh accepted a life pension 'in exchange for compliance with the British government' and died a pauper in 1893.

20.– D. China

21.– A. Virginia – The Virginia Company was formed in 1606 with the object of developing a colony on the eastern coast of America.

22.– B. Slave owners – The British government paid £20 million, the equivalent of around £17 billion today, to slave owners in compensation for the 'capital' they had lost freeing slaves.

23.– D. 2015 – The British Treasury tweeted in 2018: 'The amount of money borrowed for the Slavery Abolition Act was so large that it wasn't paid off until 2015.' Which means that living British citizens helped pay to end the slave trade. Many were outraged that slave owners' descendants were still being compensated.

24.– C. Barbados

25.– A. 99 per cent – Currently only around 80,000 artefacts are on display to the public at the British Museum in London. This amounts to roughly 1 per cent of the institution's 8 million-strong collection of objects, which are stored in archives located at the museum's Bloomsbury site, Blythe House in west London, and Franks House in east London.

15. Animals and Pets

1.– A. Horse

2.– B. Pine marten – Pine marten are larger than polecats, which are somewhat larger than stoats, which are always larger than weasels.

3.– A. Dachshund

4.– C. Being a victim of bovine tuberculosis

5.– D. Manx – Manx cats originate from the Isle of Man, which is not and has never been part of the UK, nor is it represented at Westminster. It is a self-governing British Crown Dependency, with its own parliament, government, laws and cats without tails.

6.– D. A wife

7.– B. *Zoo Quest*

8.– C. Leech

9.– A. National Canine Defence League

10.– C. 15 per cent – Another survey found that more than a quarter of British women would rather spend Valentine's Day with their cat than their partner.

11.– B. A spaniel – Elizabeth Barrett Browning's spaniel Flush, to be exact.

12.– A. One has a long tail, the other a short tail

13.– B. Ant

14.– B. Lizard

15.– B. It was found to still be alive

16.– A. Beaver

17.– C. Chief Mouser to the Cabinet Office – Larry is the first to be given the official title, despite other cats having served in Downing Street in the past.

ANSWERS

18.– A. The horrors of war – Doctor Dolittle first appeared in the author's illustrated letters to his children, written from the trenches during the First World War when actual news, he later said, was either too horrible or too dull.

19.– D. Goldfish

20.– A. Bouncer

21.– D. Rainbow skipper

22.– C. They kept the black beetles away

23.– B. Peke – 'Writing and doting over his beloved Pekingese lap-dogs was pretty much all he did,' to quote *The New York Times* on Wodehouse.

24.– A. A streaker disrupted the gundog judging

25.– D. 'Toxic' by Britney Spears – The song was co-written by former pop star Cathy Dennis who once dated the Supervet and broke up with him in 2003, the same year the song was composed.

16. Transport

1.– B. The Circle Line

2.– A. Aldgate

3.– C. Garden Bridge

4.– C. Ring the bell continuously

5.– A. Heathrow

6.– B. 1987

7.– A. So the sun shone through it on the morning of his birthday – The theory that the rising sun passed through the tunnel on Isambard Brunel's 9 April birthday was rebutted by GWR.

8.– D. 3

9.– B. 45 seconds

10.– B. Letchworth Garden City

11.– A. 13.5 hours

12.– C. Ships – It was a major employer that hired almost entirely Protestant workers.

13.– C. 12–14 days

14.– C. To make room for Terminal Two

15.– B. 28 minutes

16.– D. West Midlands

17.– C. 34.1 miles

18.– C. 20.5mph

19.– A. To fly, to serve

20.– B. *High Life*

21.– D. Peninsular and Oriental

22.– A. *William Fawcett*

23.– D. *Hercules*

24.– C. Elizabeth I

25.– A. Gloucester

17. Brexit

1.– A. 3.5 years – Brexit was originally scheduled for 29 March 2019, but the deadline was delayed after MPs rejected the deal negotiated by then prime minister Theresa May. Britain finally withdrew from the EU at 11 p.m. on 31 January 2020.

2.– B. 3 – The European Council granted deadline extensions twice to then prime minister Theresa May, in March 2019 and April 2019, and once to Boris Johnson in October 2019.

3.- D. 'Flextension' – As one EU official said of the newly agreed deadline: 'March 29th is over. As of tonight, April 12th is the new March 29th.'

4.- D. Fish – Responding to criticism from the SNP about the toll of Brexit on Scotland's fishing industry, Rees-Moss said: 'The key thing is we've got our fish back. They're now British fish and they're better and happier fish for it.' Speaker Sir Lindsay Hoyle clarified that 'Obviously, there's no overwhelming evidence for that.'

5.- C. £39 billion – Initially estimated as £39 billion under Theresa May's deal, the cost of Britain's divorce from the EU is now put at around £33 billion.

6.- A. Led by Donkeys – The group of past and present Greenpeace employees formed independently in late 2018 but remain anonymous.

7.- A. Paris – The twenty-seven member states of the European Banking Authority chose to relocate the headquarters to Paris after two rounds of voting and a drawing of lots.

8.- B. 62 per cent – With a turnout of 67.2 per cent and 2,679,513 valid votes, Scotland voted 62 per cent Remain, with every council seeing Remain majorities. Leave won the majority of votes in England and Wales, however.

9.- C. Michel Barnier – Barnier, former vice-president of the European Commission and former French Minister, was appointed by president Jean-Claude Juncker, who said: 'I wanted an experienced politician for this difficult job.'

10.– B. £350 million a week

11.– A. 'Stronger, Safer and Better Off'

12.– A. Liam Fox – The former Secretary of State for International Trade made the comments on BBC Radio 4's *Today* programme in 2017.

13.– B. Their curve

14.– A. Turkey – Michael Gove and the Vote Leave campaign said Turkey could achieve full membership of the EU by 2020, even though France and Germany were vocal about not wanting Turkey to join.

15.– C. 1973 – The United Kingdom applied to join the EU in 1961 and 1967, under Conservative prime minister Harold Macmillan, but were twice rejected by French president Charles de Gaulle. According to de Gaulle, there were certain irregularities in the UK's economic policies which made them incompatible with the EU. The UK finally became officially part of the European Economic Community (EEC) in 1973, under Conservative prime minister Edward Heath – and after de Gaulle's presidency was over.

16.– A. Only the UK – The others in this list counted as 'overseas countries and territories of the EU', as territories of members.

17.– B. Paragliding

18.– D. The Windsor Framework – The agreement was named after the meeting of the UK prime minister Rishi Sunak and the president of the European Commission, Ursula von der Leyen, at the Fairmont Hotel at Windsor Great Park.

19.– A. Noel Gallagher – Noel Gallagher said he applied for his Irish passport 'immediately after the vote, to make my life easier' when touring around Europe: 'Could I see myself living in Ireland one day? Maybe. I'll live f***ing anywhere really.'

20.– B. Increased substantially

21.– A. 3 – Three of these are 'new' trade agreements: the European Union, Japan, and an enhanced agreement with Iceland, Liechtenstein and Norway. The remaining thirty-three are continuity agreements.

22.– C. 'Chaos with Ed Miliband'

23.– C. 53 per cent – Versus 32 per cent who stood by it.

24.– B. L. K. Bennett

25.– D. All of the above – Why pick one historical example when you can pick all of them?

18. Etiquette and Customs

1.– D. 'Almost entirely white' – The rules are very precise: 'Competitors must be dressed in suitable tennis attire that is almost entirely white, from the point at which the player enters the court surround.'

2.– C. When it becomes impossible for Tottenham to finish above Arsenal – Arsenal fans celebrated St Totteringham's Day in April 2023 for the first time since the 2015–16 season.

3.– A. The Red Lion – According to Historic UK, the popularity of Red Lion pubs dates back to the time of James I and VI of Scotland, who ordered that the heraldic red lion of Scotland should be displayed on all important buildings – including pubs.

4.– B. High Street – An analysis of more than 2 million British street names found that High Street had a narrow lead over Station Road and Main Road, with 16,593, 11,521 and 7,623 entries respectively.

5.– D. Receiving an angry telling-off from their manager – The 'hairdryer treatment' of shouting at someone at close quarters rose to prominence with Sir Alex Ferguson and his infamously temperamental management of Manchester United.

6.– D. Scotland – Scotland enforced the smoking ban in 2006, when around a quarter of the population smoked. England, Wales and Northern Ireland followed the next year.

7.– A. Cèilidh – The Scots cèilidh or Irish céilí originated in the Gaelic areas of Scotland and Ireland and are similar to the Cornish Troyl tradition and the Twmpath and Noson Lawen events in Wales.

8.– B. The days of the week – 'Monandaeg' is Old English for 'day of the moon' and the origin of 'Monday'. The rest of the days of the week evolved similarly.

9.– D. You may not leave a dog in the driver's seat of a vehicle, even if it's parked – Section 12 of the Licensing Act of 1872 declares this being 'found drunk on any highway or other public place, whether a building or not, or any licensed premises' to be an offence – inclusive of every pub in England and Wales.

10.– C. Between 3 p.m. and 5 p.m. – In Victorian England, it was seen as poor taste for visitors to arrive earlier than 3 p.m.

11.– A. *Teletubbies* – Aspiring Special Branch officers had marks on their entrance exam deducted for failing to identify the four Teletubbies by name (Po, Laa-laa, Tinky Winky and Dipsy, obviously).

12.– B. Charles Darwin – A reflection of Darwin's misspent student days at Cambridge University, the Glutton Club was said to have been ended abruptly by a brown owl carcass.

13.– A. White wedding dresses – Before Queen Victoria's wedding to Prince Albert in 1840, wedding dresses commonly came in a variety of colours. The couple also popularized Christmas trees in Britain.

14.– C. Up and down – According to Twinings, the 'proper' way to stir is to place the spoon at a 12 o'clock position in the cup and softly fold the liquid back and forth two or three times to the 6 o'clock position – and to never, ever leave the teaspoon in the cup. When your teaspoon isn't being used, pop it on the saucer, to the right of the cup.

15.– D. None of the above – There's no upper age limit for serving on a jury, but you can be excused from jury service if you're 71 years of age or older and you don't want to serve on a jury.

16.– C. *Observer* – The *Observer*, first published on 4 December 1791, was the world's first Sunday newspaper and is still published today, even as Sunday circulations have fallen across the board.

17.– D. Forks – Forks were popular among Italian merchants by the fourteenth century, and were spreading through France, but British men opted to eat with their fingers. Even the Roman Catholic Church declared forks an indulgence.

18.– A. The 'females' carried machine guns, while the 'males' had cannons attached – In 1918 the decision was made that tanks should carry both heavy armament and lighter machine guns – or, as it was articulated, 'hermaphrodite'.

19.– B. The pips – The six short tones, broadcast at one-second intervals, have been generated by the BBC since 1924 to mark the precise start of every hour.

20.– C. The House of Commons – The reigning monarch cannot set foot in England's House of Commons, only their representative – though the penalty for breaches is unclear. The idea that the sovereign has to seek permission from the mayor to enter the City of London is a widespread misunderstanding.

21.– D. An abrupt and often terminal reversal in attraction to a partner – If you've 'got the ick', you are abruptly turned off by your romantic partner. In 2017, YouGov found that only 3 per cent of Brits surveyed could correctly define the term while 83 per cent had no idea what it meant.

22.– A. Dinner – Of YouGov's 42,000-odd respondents, 57 per cent call the evening meal dinner, 36 per cent opt for tea and 5 per cent say supper, though there was a clear North/South divide.

23.– A. 7 per cent – Seven per cent of Britons attend private schools, and just 1 per cent graduate from Oxford and Cambridge – yet, says the Social Mobility Commission, 'power rests with [this] narrow section of the population'.

24.– C. Whether British Asians who supported their country of ancestry in cricket against England could actually be considered British – Speaking to the *Los Angeles Times* in 1990, Tebbit said: 'A large proportion of Britain's Asian population fail to pass the cricket test', cheering for India or Pakistan, even when they played against England. The remark was predictably provocative but no more so than Lord Tebbit's other opinions.

25.– D. Laugh out loud – Laughing was considered uncouth for men and women for centuries.

19. The Other Countries

1.– D. 1707 – The Acts of Union, passed by the English and Scottish Parliaments in 1707, led to the creation of a united kingdom to be called 'Great Britain'.

2.– A. A potato pancake – A boxty is a savoury potato pancake, often included in a full Irish fry-up – as is soda bread.

3.– B. 55 per cent – There were just over 2 million votes (55.3 per cent) against Scottish independence, versus 1.6 million votes, or 44.7 per cent in favour.

4.– C. Ceres – Begun in 1314, the Ceres Games in Fife are considered the oldest continuous Highland Games in Scotland.

5.– A. Haggis – Robert Burns wrote 'Address to a Haggis' as a tribute to Scottish identity, culture and political struggle – as well as, of course, the savoury pudding.

6.– B. Castles – Wales has over 600 castles in about 8,023 square miles of land, which works out to be roughly one castle per

13 square miles: more than anywhere in Europe, and potentially the world.

7.– A. Owen Tudor – Owen Tudor, a Welsh courtier born in 1400 in Anglesey, was the grandfather of Henry VII, founder of the Tudor dynasty.

8.– D. The 1994 ceasefire in the Irish Civil War – The August 1994 ceasefire by the Provisional IRA occurs in the penultimate episode of *Derry Girls* season two.

9.– C. Catherine Zeta-Jones – Zeta-Jones and her husband, Michael Douglas, own a mansion in Mumbles, Swansea, overlooking the lighthouse.

10.– C. Snowdonia – Snowdonia, or Eryri National Park, is the largest national park in Wales. The Cambrian Mountains' bid for national park status was rejected in 1973, while campaigns for a Cambrian Mountains national park in Mid Wales are ongoing.

11.– B. Cerys Matthews – As founding member of Catatonia, alongside Super Furry Animals' Dafydd Ieuan, Cerys Matthews was a leading figure in the 'Cool Cymru' movement of the late 1990s.

12.– A. St Davids – St Davids, or Dewisland, is no bigger than a village but was granted city status in 1995.

13.– C. 58 – The UK's longest place name reads in full: Llanfairpwllgwyngyllgogerychwyrndrobwllllantysiliogogogoch. Although typed as fifty-eight characters, it has only fifty letters, because in Welsh ll, ng and ch are treated as single letters.

14.– B. Leeks – Leeks and daffodils are both national symbols of Wales to this day, but St David opted for leeks for the soldiers' helmets.

15.– A. Cheese – The vegetarian Glamorgan sausage is traditionally made of cheese, leeks and breadcrumbs.

16.– C. 15 per cent – The most recent annual population survey found that 15 per cent of the Welsh population aged three or older spoke the language daily. Thirty-three per cent could understand spoken Welsh, 26 per cent could read it and 27 per cent could write it.

17.– A. Scotland – The unicorn is Scotland's national animal, introduced to the royal coat of arms around the mid-1500s.

18.– D. Glasgow – From the mid-eighteenth century Glasgow was a major port for the rum, sugar and tobacco trades.

19.– A. Aberdeen – Aberdeen is also known as the 'Silver City', with at least 50 per cent of its buildings built from locally quarried granite.

20.– D. Armagh – The smallest county in Northern Ireland is county Armagh, at 484 square miles in area, though the smallest county in the entire island of Ireland is Louth, just 316 square miles in area.

21.- B. James Craig – The office of Prime Minister of Northern Ireland was abolished when direct rule was transferred to London in 1973.

22.- A. 'Ourselves' / 'We ourselves' – Though frequently translated as 'Ourselves alone', 'Sinn Féin' is Irish for 'Ourselves' or 'We ourselves'.

23.- C. Lagan – The River Lagan, or Abhainn an Lagáin, travels up to 53 miles from Slieve Croob mountain in County Down to its mouth at Belfast Lough and into the Irish Sea.

24.- A. Apple – The greasy pippin is an Irish-heritage variety of apple described as having crisp, refreshing, cream flesh.

25.- D. France – Scotland's Auld Alliance with France, in 1295, proved disastrous when in 1513 England's King Henry VIII declared war on France – prompting Scotland's King James IV to invade England. England declared victory over Scotland in the Battle of Flodden that same year.

20. Brits Abroad

1.- C. Phil Collins – In January 2000 Phil Collins appeared alongside Christina Aguilera, Enrique Iglesias and Toni Braxton in this Disney-produced halftime event for Superbowl 34, performing his song for the *Tarzan* movie (also a Disney production).

2.- A. Canada and the US – The first international cricket game was played between the US and Canada on the grounds of the St

George's Cricket Club in New York in 1844. The English play-ers' inaugural tour of North America followed in 1859.

3.– C. Robbie Coltrane – Coltrane may not have cameoed on *Friends*, but he did appear in the (far superior) *Frasier*.

4.– A. Nigeria – Four Guinness breweries are located in Nigeria, explaining its popularity in the country. Two more are located in Ghana and Cameroon.

5.– B. D C United – Rooney joined D C United of Major League Soccer from Everton in 2018, before leaving in 2020 to join Derby County as player and coach.

6.– D. Owen Hargreaves – Hargreaves was born in Canada and grew up in Germany but was eligible to play for England because his father is English (his mother is Welsh).

7.– A. When the setting sun is framed by skyscrapers – Astrophysicist Neil deGrasse Tyson coined the term 'Manhattanhenge' in 1997 to describe the alignment of the sun with the city's grid.

8.– B. One in ten – According to figures quoted by Boris Johnson in 2016, some 5 to 6 million Brits now live abroad: evidence of a 'formidable exporter of human talent'.

9.– B. 5 per cent – The most popular destinations for Brits emigrat-ing in the early twentieth century were Canada, Australia, New Zealand and South Africa – though many did eventually return.

10.– A. South Africa – By the mid-1890s, Cornish miners reportedly made up a quarter of the white workforce in the mines on the Rand.

11.– A. New York – The English muffin was invented by Samuel Bath Thomas after his relocation to New York City in 1874. By 1880, Thomas had his own bakery in the neighbourhood now known as Chelsea.

12.– B. 'When the Levee Breaks' – Though Led Zeppelin popularized the song, 'When the Levee Breaks' was first recorded by Memphis Minnie and Kansas Joe McCoy in 1929 – proof of the back-and-forth across the Atlantic.

13.– D. Adele – Adele has won sixteen Grammys, putting her just behind Sting and Eric Clapton, both with seventeen, and Paul McCartney with eighteen. Adele is also the most-awarded female foreign act in the award's history.

14.– B. Failed In London, Try Hong Kong – Pre-dating the handover of Hong Kong to China in 1999, the acronym FILTH captured the tendency of multinational corporations to send under-performing or out-of-favour employees offshore.

15.– D. Sussex – Imran Khan played for Sussex from 1983 to 1988, after making his Test cricket debut for Pakistan – and against England – in June 1971.

ANSWERS

16.– D. Was reassuring about spiders – The episode was removed from broadcast by the ABC for misleading children by saying that 'spiders can't hurt you'.

17.– B. *Hamlet* – Directed, adapted by, and starring Laurence Olivier, *Hamlet* remains the only Shakespearean adaptation to have won the Best Picture Oscar – in 1948.

18.– C. Spain – In 2022, UK residents made an estimated 16.5 million trips to Spain, of 71.8 million in total.

19.– B. Alcoholism – On the subject of Brits' love of 'strong drink', the Oxford Survey of the British Empire continued: 'many still consume more than is physiologically good for them'.

20.– A. Petula Clark – While performing with Harry Belafonte, the 'Downtown' singer Petula Clark touched his arm: the first time that a white woman had touched a Black man on television, causing a vehement backlash from sponsors.

21.– A. The tax rate – Michael Caine moved to the US after the tax rate on top earners was increased to 83 per cent under James Callaghan's Labour government. He returned when Margaret Thatcher came into power in 1979.

22.– C. *Evita* – Tim Rice's frequent collaborator Andrew Lloyd Webber is also an EGOT winner.

23.– D. Eddie Redmayne – Actor Eddie Redmayne was born in Westminster, London (then he went to Eton with Prince William).

24.– B. The Teletubbies – The Teletubbies visited New York City to celebrate their tenth anniversary and revealed their true identities for the first time.

25.– D. Anthony Horowitz – Anthony Horowitz has only written about MI6, not worked for it . . . as far as we know.